Published by Advantage, Charleston, South Carolina.
Member of Advantage Media Group.

ADVANTAGE is a registered trademark and the Advantage colophon is a trademark of
Advantage Media Group, Inc.

Printed in the United States of America.

ISBN: 978-159932-428-9
LCCN: 2014953412

Book design by George Stevens.
Photography © Chipper Hatter.

This publication is designed to provide accurate and authoritative information in regard
to the subject matter covered. It is sold with the understanding that the publisher is not
engaged in rendering legal, accounting, or other professional services. If legal advice
or other expert assistance is required, the services of a competent professional person
should be sought.

This book is intended to express the views and opinions of the author and is neither
written as, nor should be interpreted to be, professional advice regarding code
compliance, safety, engineering, financial or other matters. The advice contained
herein may not be suitable for every situation, and readers should retain licensed
professional(s) and consult authorities, codes, covenants, and regulations before starting
any construction project.

Advantage Media Group is proud to be a part of the Tree Neutral®
program. Tree Neutral offsets the number of trees consumed in the
production and printing of this book by taking proactive steps such as
planting trees in direct proportion to the number of trees used to print
books. To learn more about Tree Neutral, please visit www.treeneutral.
com. To learn more about Advantage's commitment to being a
responsible steward of the environment, please visit www.
advantagefamily.com/green

The Forever Home

How to work with an architect to design the home of your dreams

KEVIN HARRIS

TABLE OF CONTENTS

TABLE OF CONTENTS

An outdoor fireplace stages this cozy gathering area. A classic bed swing delights and invites snuggles and warm memories. This space is a sacred place for solitary contemplation, a respite to unwind, enjoy and appreciate the outdoors.

The Forever Home

"There's no place like *home*."

—DOROTHY, *THE WIZARD OF OZ*

For most of us there really is no place like home. But like Dorothy, even though we want to go there and may have the resources to get there, we still need someone to show us the way. The purpose of this book is to provide a foundation that will empower you, the reader, to make your journey to your "forever home" and to detail how an architect can be an indispensable guide.

What is a forever home? It's the home you've always dreamed of—one that fits so well it becomes a part of your identity, a place that nurtures your spirits and houses your most precious earthly belongings, including your family and possessions. You may leave to visit other beautiful places, but whenever you return, you know you are truly home.

Designed by renowned architect A. Hays Town, this Bevelo Lamp's classic shadow dances across a veranda where Lamb's tongue chamfers transform an otherwise indelicate square columns into a softer assembly of octagonal faces.

From an architect's perspective, a forever home is designed with the thought and care not only to accommodate your current needs, but with the anticipation of how it will support your life going forward. It means deliberately designing spaces and selecting materials that optimize livability for you, your children, grandchildren, aging parents, and even you, in your later years. I call this design approach "grace in place."

The Value of Architectural Guidance

If you're contemplating building, renovating, or redesigning a home, whether it's your current home, your next home, or your forever home, you'll need help. My architectural role is to help you create the home you want, and I wrote this book to be a guide that will help you reach that goal.

I have been a residential architect for more than three decades. The experience I've gained in that time has given me a deep understanding of the concerns, fears, and dreams people typically have regarding the construction or renovation of a home. The questions I hear are familiar ones: Where do I start? What is the process? How do I protect myself? How do I put together the team I'll need to get it done? And so on.

Over the years, the size and scope of my firm's projects have increased along with my experience, but what has remained constant is my commitment to helping and educating my clients, even when they were just potential clients.

Early in my full-time practice, I began to offer design consultations to people who were considering building a new home or renovating an existing home. During these house calls we would discuss items specific to their vision, of course, but a lot of time was spent reviewing the different options for design and construction, the pros and cons of each, the factors that influence the decisions on both accounts, what to expect during the process, and how to prepare for the journey. The first phase of our conversation

Wrap around verandas and an elevated foundation create an elegant home that resonates with the Southern culture.

always included architectural discussions, but it also began an educational process that continued until my clients moved into their new home.

Each month in the United States, between six and seven hundred thousand new homes are built. According to the statistics, the vast majority are designed without an architect. Is this representative of the cultural disconnect between the architectural profession and

the residential consumer? Or is it, rather, due more to a lack of exposure to an understanding of what architects actually do? I believe it is a bit of both, but either way, the numbers underscore the lack of professional influence architects have on the marketplace, and the potentials of increasing their role. More information must be made readily accessible to empower existing homeowners, future homeowners, and potential remodelers about the process of home design and construction, and of the value prospect of engaging an architect.

As of this writing, there are more than 100,000 registered architects in the United States, but only a fraction practice custom residential design. Considering the millions of homes built or remodeled each year, it's easy to see why there is a greater demand for residential design services than architects alone can satisfy. It's also really no surprise that many people don't even know an architect, much less understand what they bring to a project.

Creating a home that sustains and supports the life of the family that dwells in it is a priceless endeavor. It's where much of our lives are spent, where we eat, sleep, grow, love, nurture, and form bonds. A home is part of the American dream, as deeply entrenched in

Historic research guided this authentic composition that captures the majesty of houses along St. Charles Avenue in New Orleans.

My Own Architectural Journey

I was five years old when I first knew I wanted to be an architect. It happened when my father's cousin, an architect, came to help renovate our typical, suburban, ranch-styled home. His name was Roy Guderian and he worked with the legendary Frank Lloyd Wright at Taliesin. For an entire year, "Uncle" Roy drew plans and then supervised construction at our home.

I was constantly underfoot, and enthralled with it all–the drawings and blueprints, the pencils and erasers, the construction work, and all the sights and sounds I experienced watching our environment change and grow. Architecture became my first love.

Fast-forward 13 years to when I entered Louisiana State University (LSU) as a first-year architecture major. The trend in undergraduate school at the time was to throw off the "constraints" of traditional design and embrace the clean, unadorned, and uncluttered regimen of modernism, which I did, becoming an apostle of architectural reductionism, a disciple of disembellishment.

A few years after that, I was accepted into Harvard University's Graduate School of Design, where one of my professors was

Florentine elements in limestone echo the architecture of the owner's
alma mater and maintain the neighborhood's integrity.

the esteemed Moshe Safdie. For my first project, I proudly rendered a thoroughly modern architectural plan with zero cultural references. Safdie took one look and said, "Well, Mr. Harris, I see in two weeks at Harvard you managed to throw away 4,000 years of architectural history."

I was stunned and, as a consequence, unshackled from my undergraduate emphasis on avoiding all cultural or regional influences that would negate the universal ideals of modern architecture. I realized that an architecture for every place and every culture was also an architecture of no place and of no culture. No longer did I feel compelled to avoid the vernacular, the common language of style native to any region. I no longer felt prohibited from including stylistic and cultural references in my work.

After completing my degree and working for a few years in Boston, I returned to LSU where I taught in the department of architecture. During this period, I also began a private practice, overseeing home renovation projects.

I loved the challenge. No two homes were built exactly alike or even used the same construction sequences. I discovered the satisfaction and joy that comes from preserving the fabric of older neighborhoods, weaving new life and texture into existing homes while maintaining the bonds of the surrounding neighborhoods.

On a professor's salary, and as a father of three young daughters, I was also happy for the supplemental income. More importantly, the projects I accepted—porch additions, minor façade facelifts, and the like—allowed me to hone my skills as a practicing (versus theoretical) architect.

A decade later, I left teaching and began my architectural practice full-time. Over the years, the size and scope of my projects have steadily increased, along with my own professional growth and development. And with that experience I have gained an understanding of how intimate the design of a home is, and how intensely personal it can be.

I love what I do and I love working with my clients and their families. To many of their children now, I'm "Uncle Kevin," helping them to create the home they will grow to love.

Uncle Roy would be proud.

our society's collective psyche as baseball and apple pie. For two-thirds of American families, it also represents their single largest asset.

For something this central, this critical to our lives, I believe that people deserve access to information about how it all happens. I believe that the most successful project results from the synergy of an informed and empowered client, a professional and experienced architect, and a skillful and knowledgeable builder. This book aims to put to rest the idea that architectural help is beyond the reach of most would-be homeowners, builders, and remodelers, and to make a case for what architects actually do, and highlight the value proposition they can provide.

Fair Warning: This Book Has a Point of View

I decided to write this book from a very distinct point of view—my own—based on over 40 years of formal architectural education and hands-on practice. It is meant to provide you, the reader, with the same information and knowledge that I have shared with hundreds of clients, friends, and family to aid them in successfully achieving their forever homes.

A sympathetic addition maintains the rustic Tudor charm of this cottage while doubling its size. Drawings on page 139.

No single book can cover everything. And even if it could, who would want to read all that? What's here is what I have successfully taught clients, again and again, year after year.

I know that a home is more than mere shelter. It is a sacred space for the life of a family, a place where the occupants should feel at peace. I believe that a home supports individuals or families best when it functions for its intended purpose, whatever that may be.

When it comes to architectural design, I also strongly believe in proportion and know that there is a rhythm and pattern in nature that feels right to the eye and resonates with the soul. I want to bring that sensitivity to the work I do. I want to give homeowners the opportunity to embrace what is uniquely their personality and to find a way to express that in the built environment.

I would like my clients to consider me as a guide on their journey, a trusted advisor—perhaps even an "uncle" Kevin who tells it as he sees it. I demonstrate the architect-led design process in this book as practiced by my office. Of course, you are always free to disagree or see things differently. Other firms' practice models may vary. However, what you find here will help inform your choices.

New columns, doors, and dormers supply proportional elegance, visual gravity, and daylight to this cottage. Drawings on page 142.

And, after reading this book, you should be able to:

➢ Recognize the architect-led design process as practiced in my office

➢ Differentiate and assess the trade-offs, pros, and cons of the various design service options

➢ Collect the information and resources needed to lay the groundwork for designing a forever home

➢ Discover or refine your own style and bring your own distinct culture to the process

➢ Demonstrate your design preferences in collected images

➢ Identify and assemble a team of professionals

➢ Trace the flow of design through construction, and distinguish the various roles and responsibilities of key players

A master suite and balcony above the new kitchen and family room capture a relaxed, West Indies atmosphere.

➢ Evaluate the potential of renovation as an alternative to new construction

➢ Appraise the factors that govern building costs and their interrelationship

Let the journey begin!

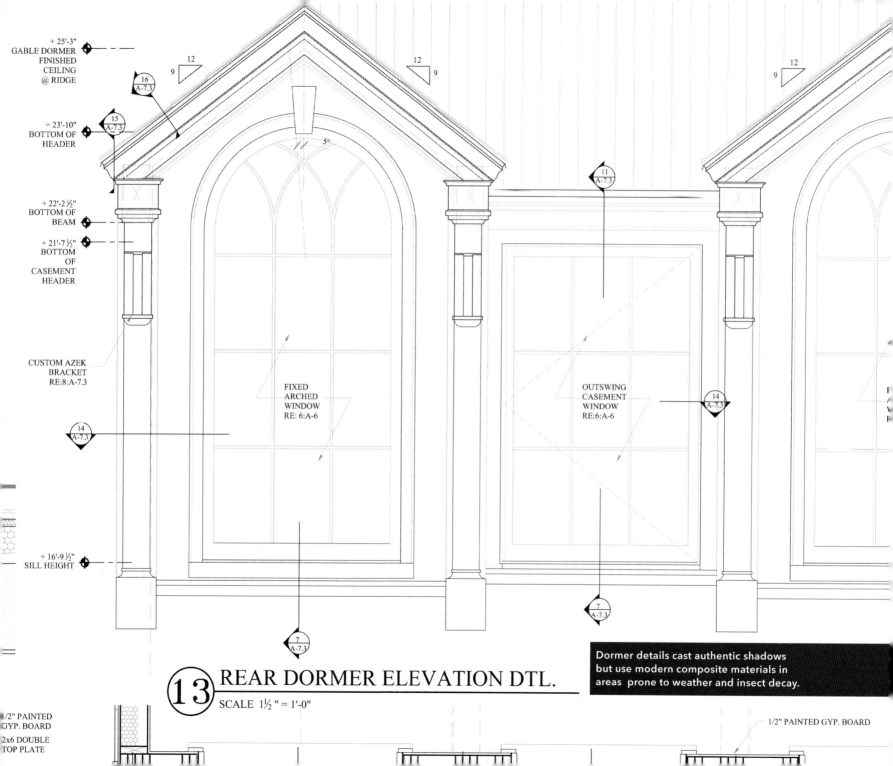

+ 25'-3"
GABLE DORMER
FINISHED
CEILING
@ RIDGE

+ 23'-10"
BOTTOM OF
HEADER

+ 22'-2 ½"
BOTTOM OF
BEAM

+ 21'-7 ½"
BOTTOM
OF
CASEMENT
HEADER

CUSTOM AZEK
BRACKET
RE:8:A-7.3

+ 16'-9 ½"
SILL HEIGHT

16 / A-7.3

15 / A-7.3

11 / A-7.3

14 / A-7.3

14 / A-7.3

12   9

12   9

12   9

5°

FIXED
ARCHED
WINDOW
RE: 6:A-6

OUTSWING
CASEMENT
WINDOW
RE:6:A-6

7 / A-7.3

7 / A-7.3

13 REAR DORMER ELEVATION DTL.

SCALE 1 ½ " = 1'-0"

Dormer details cast authentic shadows
but use modern composite materials in
areas prone to weather and insect decay.

1/2" PAINTED
GYP. BOARD

2x6 DOUBLE
TOP PLATE

1/2" PAINTED GYP. BOARD

CHAPTER ONE

Your Architect

"No one is really an architect.
That's just a job they make up for movies."

—THE MINDY PROJECT

What's an Architect Anyway?

An architect is someone who has studied, trained, and become licensed in the planning, design, and construction of buildings and their surrounding spaces. The word *architect* came from the Latin *architectus*, which in turn originated from the Greek *arkhitekton*, or "chief builder." We do exist, and not only in movies. Since this book addresses how an architect can help you realize your forever home, it's important to understand that in the construction industry, the name *architect* has a specific legal meaning beyond the dictionary definition.

Details make the difference. An architect is trained to create drawings that guide construction and meet needs for functionality, durability, and style.

In the United States no professionals in the building industry may call themselves architects unless they are licensed in that state or territorial jurisdiction. There are three major steps to becoming an architect: rigorous university education, professional internship, and seven rigorous exams. Each US jurisdiction sets individual requirements, and several allow exceptions.

Architecture is a complex and challenging area of study, and licensure requires at least 10 years of concentrated effort. Students attend programs sanctioned by the National Architectural Accreditation Board. These take from five to eight years to complete. Following graduation, candidates complete a directed internship of 5,600 hours that, on average, consume an additional five years.

In addition, there are seven stringent exams on programming, site planning, building design, construction systems, structural and building systems, construction documents, and contracts. The title of architect is then granted by individual jurisdictions on a one- or two-year basis. Renewal of the title requires annual continuing education. Architects must be life-long learners whose knowledge and understanding of the built environment is continually updated.

What Does an Architect Do (in General)?

In the United States, individual states license architects to practice. In my state of Louisiana, the statute states that I am licensed to "provide services in connection with the design, construction, enlargement, or alterations of buildings, or the space within and surrounding buildings, which have human occupancy or habitation as their principal purpose."

That is one general description of what we do, but, in laymen's terms, I would say that architects consult with owners to determine the functions, purpose, aesthetic preferences, and desired materials to incorporate into a design. They create sketches, models, and illustrations that depict the proposed building, and create detailed drawings and written specifications that guide the pricing, procurement, scheduling, and sequencing of construction. They offer services that provide conceptual ideas and details, and they assist you with the various stages of the process, from obtaining a permit through construction.

What Does an Architect Who Specializes in Residences Do?

An architect can help you decide what to build and how to build it. He can advise you in selecting a builder, assist with permitting, and act as your agent through construction.

NOT JUST DRAWINGS

An architect does more than prepare blueprints. Drawings *are* involved; however, the significant value of a set prepared by an architect becomes clearer with an understanding of what they do. Drawings are necessary, but they only describe what and how to build, assuming what was drawn will actually meet your needs for functionality, durability, and style. To assure a successful venture, these documents must integrate a thousand individual decisions and selections into a cohesive whole. Tailoring a house from scratch, customized to your specific preferences, is an involved process, and an architect safeguards these design and selection decisions against common mistakes, misinterpretations, and random changes by others during construction. You are also spared from the vulnerability and pressure of having to make and enforce your wishes and intents amid the confusion, immediacy, and dust of construction activities. An architect is well versed in the construction process and will guide you through many choices while preparing the blueprints.

A less expensive option is the preparation of construction drawings in which many decisions are predetermined—for example, limiting the customization options to minor plan adjustments, finish materials, colors, fixtures, and appliances. However, no set of plans and specifications are assembly instructions. Drawings can only serve as a guide. Anyone who has experienced construction knows very well the multitude of questions, proposals, and decisions involved over and above what appears on the drawings. An architect acts in your best interest throughout the construction process, observes the construction, administers your contract with the contractor, and determines when construction work does not comply with the plans or is otherwise unacceptable. The architect's additional clarification, guidance, and expert judgment during construction helps prevent questions and issues from becoming bigger problems, headaches, or expensive surprises.

WHAT TO BUILD: SCHEMATIC DESIGN

Deciding what to build is challenging, but it is an area in which architects excel. Analytical and artistic processes are combined to create a guide to what should be included while exploring alternatives—for example, suggesting where to consider higher quality materials or products to reduce maintenance costs or increase per-

1   HER CLOSET

2   HIS CLOSET

3   MASTER BATH

4   MASTER BATH

5   FOYER

6   KITCHEN

7   HIS OFFICE

A sheet of interior details illustrate the high level of attention required to create a forever home.

sonal comfort and enjoyment. Your architect ushers you through the creative process and shows, on paper, how your ideas should look. Your architect can also help you assemble and coordinate the additional design team members to guide the planning of complementary interiors, artwork, and landscaping.

HOW TO BUILD: DETAILED DRAWINGS

Your ideas need to be communicated to those responsible for construction. This translation requires a conversion into a specific language that can be clearly and unmistakably understood by the craftsmen.

An architect transforms your what-to-build schematics into detailed instructions for constructing each part: materials, size, placement, quality, and finish. Builders and their craftsmen easily reproduce the most common details following minimal guidance and basic drawings. However, betting on them to blindly produce specialty items becomes a dicey gamble. Builders can only be expected to build what they have already mastered. Their

repertoire of excellence will expand to include most customization challenges, provided drawings sufficiently describe the unique characteristics, and the author is available for questions and clarifications.

WHO SHOULD BUILD

Selecting the contractor who is best for your project, your personality, and your budget should be based upon more than price. It is paramount that you choose someone you trust, based on reputation and experience, someone who promises a fair price, quality equal to or above expectations, and a reasonable time frame for completion of the work. Your architect will suggest what to consider in a contractor and provide a short list to begin interviews.

Design Service Alternatives

Most houses built each year use plans prepared by non-architects. These homes may be constructed with house plans from a do-it-yourself computer program or a plan book. The plans may be drawn up by a drafting service, someone who attended architectural school, an interior designer, a contractor with a drafting background, or an architect. How can you distinguish one option from the other? How is using an architect different?

THE BEST OPTION IS THE ONE MOST APPROPRIATE

Choosing between good and bad design services requires that you understand what is appropriate, or not, for producing the results you desire for an acceptable price. The more familiar you become with the specific alternatives, the more what first appear as subtle distinctions become determining factors. This is also the case when purchasing a car, ball gown, or having a photograph taken.

Cars are offered through the Internet, neighbors, used lots, and dealerships. Some make it an event and purchase their vehicles directly from the factory, only to ship home their vehicle after driving through Europe.

> "The more familiar you become with the specific alternatives, the more what first appear as subtle distinctions become determining factors."

While each results in a car, the only similarity in each method is the noun *car*. The buying experience, cost, and offerings vary significantly. Considerations include the amount of due diligence and background research done on the recommended vendor, the type and quality of vehicle, and the ability of the seller to stand behind the product. No option is good or bad on its face as each fulfills the basic function of transportation: getting you from point A to point B. It is the additional features that drive the selection preference. For a teenager's first car, you may consider a 10-year-old compact, for sale by owner, and with a mileage of 150,000. If driving to work, you may prefer a newer model with less mileage and greater reliability. When you feel financially secure, you are more likely to shop at a reputable dealership than from newspaper ads. When ready for your dream car, a vacation trip to Europe is a possibility.

Photographs in this age of technology can capture images of your child through numerous ways: from your phone camera, at a studio located in a big box mall, from a private photographer, or by commissioning a portrait artist. Each option delivers an image of your child. However, is a selfie better than a custom portrait? It depends on the intended application. Is the image intended for sharing on social media or for gracing your walls for years to come? Costs for the image can be lowered when less effort or skill is required, and increased for more artistry and customization. The final price should parallel the education, skill, and reputation of the photographer. In the end, balance the desired quality level with the budget.

Dresses and ball gowns are likewise crafted for the intended use. My wife and I live in Louisiana and attend numerous black-tie, white-tie, debutante, and Mardi Gras balls each year. How much energy—and budget—we invest in choosing what to wear depends on the relative importance of that event and our disposable income. My wife has worn borrowed gowns, thrift store outfits, and designer rack pieces. For each of our daughter's debutante balls, the importance of the event was greater and more was invested in finding an appropriate dress. One friend and neighbor crafts beautiful couture gowns, and a fellow Rotarian styles men's suits from the finest fabrics, following the latest fashion. Their products are custom tailored, finely crafted, impressively beautiful, and expensive, as are most things that are well made and thoughtfully designed. When the occasion warrants appearing at your very best, these clothes are well worth the investment.

Similar to deciding how to acquire a car, photograph, or ball gown, there are many ways to obtain a set of drawings. The term *plan* often marks where the similarities end. The best option for your home is the one that appropriately balances your objectives, desires, and budget.

THE OPTIONS

➤ *Prepare the plans yourself:* You can do this provided you have the structural knowledge and drafting ability to generate a set of plans for permitting and construction. Computer programs abound that suggest anyone can design a home. And we all can in the sense we are not prohibited from doing so. However, few have the actual skill set to create sections, details, framing plans, electrical and drainage plans, and so on. Even fewer are equipped to address all of the construction, building code, and aesthetic issues that come with house design. Any effort invested in designing your own house is an education you can apply to a future project, or resort to as a heightened awareness when working with someone else. No education is wasted, and all attempts, hit or miss, will add to your understanding of home construction.

➤ *Purchase "plans" from a book:* Often referred to as stock plans, these plans are available in print or digital format. They are affordable, quickly delivered, and the options are seemingly endless. I must caution that several trade-offs come with increased affordability: Stock plans are built many times, reducing the production cost per use; they can require fewer drawings by lessening the scope of work that they describe. This leaves you or your contractor to decide many of the details, schedules, and selections, such as structural, mechanical, and electrical items. Drawings that describe these missing items will likely be required for permitting, in addition to a site plan that locates utility easements, building setbacks, site drainage, and so on. Stock plans are also one-size-fits-all plans. Any customization or adjustments, if available, will cost extra. So while book plans are good for getting ideas, you will likely need help to make these plans buildable. If your building site is located outside a municipality and not subject to the requirements or safety benefits of building permits and inspectors, I caution to be certain to select craftsmen you trust to prudently apply their local knowledge and experience.

➢ *Hire a designer:* A designer goes by many names including residential designer, home designer, drafting service, building designer, or almost any trade name with the term *design* in the title. Some specialize in specific areas of a home, such as a kitchen and bath designers. Working with a designer costs more and takes longer than ordering a set of stock plans. This is justified as a designer offers a more individualized service. You can direct the designer to draw exactly what you think you want. The vast majority of homes constructed in the United States follow drawings by a residential designer of some fashion. Some designers will also assist with your renovation project. However, because renovations present the challenge of unknown, additional, and hidden variables, many designers tend to shy away from them.

➢ *Engage an architect:* Work with a licensed professional to define, design, and build your home. This is, typically, the most expensive method of obtaining a set of plans, but given your needs and anticipated budget, it could be the most appropriate.

Do I Need an Architect?

I hear this question several times a week, and it's a good one, without a simple yes or no answer. It depends upon your personal idea of what determines need. Is it something you must have, or is it something you would be well advised to have?

Engaging an architect is a must when you live in a neighborhood or municipality that requires the stamp of a licensed professional for construction permitting. Otherwise, as a basic right of citizenship, states allow that anyone can design his or her own home. It is not when the designer is involved, but rather, when the construction craftsmen are involved that public safety and building codes kick in and licensed individuals are required to work on a residence. Specific installations must be made by licensed individuals such as the plumbers, electricians, and heating/air conditioning professionals. Most laws governing home design do not require an architect's involvement. So, if using an architect is not a mandate, when would you be well advised to use an architect?

YOUR FIRST HOME

If you're a young couple buying your first house—one you don't plan to live in for more than three to five years—I'll become your uncle Kevin and say, "Your best bet is to buy an existing home." This is especially true if your budget is modest. You will learn a great deal about how your starter home adapts, or not, to your developing lifestyle. In addition, any renovation to an early home to accommodate your lifestyle will give you insight into the complexities of home design. This experience will come in handy when deciding on the features, arrangements,

"Is an architect something you must have, or is it something you would be well advised to have?"

and improvements you will want to include in your next home.

WHAT TO CONSIDER AFTER THAT FIRST HOME?

What about that gray area between your starter home and your forever home? Should you use an architect? It depends. Here are multiple factors I suggest that you allow to influence your conclusion.

> *Time:* How long do you plan to stay in the home? Do you anticipate moving in three years, or do you plan on staying put for the foreseeable future? Employing an architect and building to a higher level of quality brings additional benefits and sometimes costs. The longer you live in any one place, the longer you have to experience, enjoy, and amortize the customization. This is similar to my daughters' clothing budgets. The more times (longer) my daughters can anticipate wearing an item of clothing, the more I am willing to invest in quality and design, since the cost per wear is reduced.

> *Customization:* How individual is your style? Do you dress, live, and entertain as your neighbors do? Are your needs, activities, and interests more unique than, or restricted by, currently available houses? The benefits of using an architect increase with the desire for custom solutions.

> *Experience:* What is your knowledge of design and construction? Have you built or renovated a home before? Do you have reliable resources that can guide you through the process? Can you devote enough time to become knowledgeable and proficient about construction practices? What is your comfort level with self-navigating material selections, room arrangements, contracts, and building permits?

The less you know about construction, the less time you can devote to the endeavor, and the

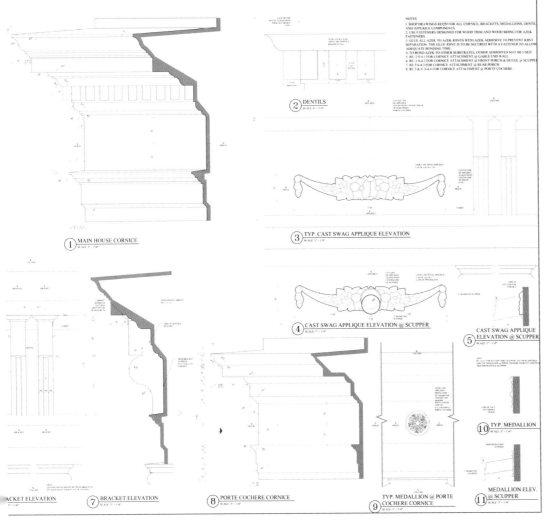

Accurate details guide modern craftsmen to re-create new features with historic authenticity.

less tolerance you have with the inevitable challenges, the more you should consider professional assistance. On the flip side, a client who renovated more than five homes said he didn't really "see" the overall design and construction process clearly until he worked with my firm.

➢ *Design:* How sensitive are you to design issues? Do you notice awkward proportions or color combinations, or do you question the artistry of certain textures? The more attuned you are to matters of design and its subtle benefits, the more you will appreciate engaging design professionals.

➢ *Investment:* What financial investment do you plan to allocate to your next home? For larger amounts, there is a point beyond which it only makes sense to use an architect. Using a sliding scale, the more you are inclined to invest, the more I advise using an architect and related designers.

➤ *Getting it right*: Do you have the time, experience, and budget, but find that you just can't seem to "get it right?" Can you visualize and articulate your desired features but remain unable to put them all together? The more important it is for you to "get it right" this time, the more you should consider taking advantage of the education and training of an experienced design professional.

WHAT ABOUT HOME REMODELING?

I advise using an architect when considering a residential renovation for the initial feasibility and conceptual solution, but not always for detailed drawings or construction observation. Architects offer a spectrum of services that can be broken down into parts, or phases. Your particular renovation may only require the services of an architect for initial design decisions, leaving the remainder of details to you and your contractor. Whether you're embarking on a complete renovation or simply adding one room, getting professional advice is the best way to avoid a blundering mistake that can ruin the look and aesthetic spirit of your home, or create problematic traffic flow problems with the floor plan. This is especially important with tight budgets where you can't afford to spend money twice—once to do it wrong and a second time to make corrections. Your best protection is to have an architect guide you to get the big decisions right the first time.

A good way to explore the initial feasibility of a renovation and define a conceptual solution is to hire an architect for a design consultation. This can be a flat fee or on an hourly basis. A design consultation is a service in which an architect comes into your home on a modern-day "house call" to meet with you for three or four hours. The architect will examine your house, review drawings and photographs you provide, listen to your likes and dislikes, talk with you about what you want to fix or accomplish, and sketch out feasible, holistic solutions. The architect will study your floor plan, the flow from room to room, the proportions, stylistic details, utility systems, and, especially in high precipitation environments, the roofline and drainage. There's nothing worse, in my opinion, than an addition that does not solve your issues, creates additional problems, and looks like a tacked-on afterthought or presents an anachronistic element that simply cries for demolition.

I created my design consultation service decades ago after realizing the incredible value produced during the initial meeting. During these brief house calls, I was able to provide firm recommendations on what to add on or how to renovate. I found that when the *what* and *where* to build had been soundly determined, and when the many details of *how* to build could be responsibly guided by what was already existing, my further involvement was not always needed.

The conclusion of the design consultation typically contains the majority of the professional guidance homeowners need to comfortably take to a contractor. The hand-drawn sketches are the homeowners' to keep and use, regardless of whether they engage my office for more detailed drawings. I often encourage clients to seriously consider engaging service providers with less horsepower and expense than an architect. For the more involved and detailed renovations, however, I strongly recommend continuing with an architect for detailed drawings and guidance during construction.

Remodeling consultations present the fascinating challenge of working with existing construction. Architects must design "inside the box" in order to arrive at an "outside-the-box," highly creative solution. Houses with the tightest constraints, from bungalows to estate properties, are often the most interesting, and no two are quite alike.

Chapter 6 specifically covers the topic of home renovation.

The "Value Proposition" of an Architect

A forever home is likely to be one of your largest financial investments. The services of an architect can go a long way toward helping create your ideal environment and protecting this asset.

Architectural services provide proven value in many ways, both tangible and intangible. Architecture is all around us, and the product of what architects do can appear simple. One common misunderstanding is the assumption that the value of an architect is to obtain a set of blueprints. The drawings produced are merely instruments of service and are only an initial manifestation. The real benefit comes from the thoughts and intentions that are described on paper and their effect on your bottom line, psyche, and the neighboring properties. Well-thought-out plans include the potential for targeted expenditures and higher appraisal values. All critical decisions will follow a neat, streamlined process, and your architect can act as your agent on the oversight of the construction. Some intangible benefits you can expect include a skillfully applied knowledge of building science and technology, the minimization of costly mistakes, inclusion of a trained aesthetic sensibility, and the creation of inspirational and healthy spaces for you to enjoy. In addition, there are a myriad of psychological dividends, increased visibility, ease of living, and a likely positive effect on surrounding property.

➢ *Licensure:* As a general rule, an architect must meet the high standards of formal education, professional internship, certification, and continuing education in order to offer services. There are many detailed and complex elements to make buildings safe, healthy, functional, and enduring. The complexity of the building process and the public's concern for safety mandates that an architect be a licensed professional.

For more on licensure, see next pages..

AIA, LEED AP, E-I-E-I-O

My father-in-law, JK, enjoyed teasing me about the initials following my name. He would smile and call me Kevin Harris, E-I-E-I-O. After hearing him joke, my young daughter nicknamed him JK, L-M-N-O-P.

In the construction industry, the letters can mean more than a friendly family nickname. Many sound alike, so it is understandable that there is confusion about the differences and distinctions. Even among industry professionals, it is a topic of debate. A quick search on the Internet can provide real-life examples of this "alphabet soup"—for example, John Doe, AIA, NCARB, AIBD, CPBD, CAPS, CGP, GCP; or Jane Doe, RA, NCARB, CSI, CDT, LEED AP BD+C; or Jack Doe, AIBD, CST, CCA.

Letters after a name are meant to convey some authority, but just how much authority is conveyed varies greatly. The letters can (1) denote licensure, (2) attest to a certification, (3) represent membership in an organization, or (4) combine licensure or certification *and* membership.

Licensure is a legal term, just like *architect*. It is a non-voluntary process whereby a governmental agency regulates a profession.

Certification is a voluntary process, typically administered by a nongovernmental organization to identify and acknowledge individuals who have met defined standards. These standards can include a combination of education, experience, and an examination of knowledge.

When you encounter someone with an "alphabet soup" of designations, look up the designations and know what they mean. Below are seven common designations found in the residential design arena. Only the first three require licensure for membership.

Letters That Indicate Licensure

The designation AIA after a name indicates membership in the American Institute of Architects. To be a member of the AIA, one must be a licensed architect. The letters FAIA stand for Fellow of the American Institute of Architects. Fellowship status is held by a small minority of AIA members and is achieved when an architect has made significant contributions to the profession of architecture.

The letters NCARB stand for the National Council of Architecture Registration Boards. The letters NCARB after a name indicate the holder is a licensed architect with NCARB certification. Only one in three architects nationwide hold this certification. NCARB reciprocity paves the way for eligibility for licensure in multiple jurisdictions including Canada, depending on each board's requirements. The NCARB also administers the Architect Registration Exam for all registration boards in the United States.

The letters RA stand for registered architect. They proclaim that the architect has completed an internship and passed the Architectural Registration Exam.

Letters That Do Not Require or Indicate Licensure

The letters AIBD stand for the American Institute of Building Design. Anyone who is a member of the AIBD may use the AIBD logo, along with the description of "member of AIBD," or "AIBD member."

The letters CPBD after someone's name means that person is a Certified Professional Building Designer. It is a title permitted by the American Institute of Building De-

	Buildings	Interiors	Plantings
State Licensure			
Accredited University Study	AIA	ASID	ASLA
Liability Insurance	**American Institute of Architects** **Architect**	**American Society of Interior Designers** **Interior Designer**	**American Society of Landscape Architects** **Landscape Architect**
Certification	**AIBD:** American Institute of Building Design **CPBD:** Certified Professional Building Designer **AIBD:** American Institute of Building Design **LEED:** Leadership in Energy & Environmental Design	**NKBA:** National Kitchen & Bath Association **AKBD:** Associate Kitchen and Bath Designer **CKBP:** Certified Kitchen and Bath Professional **CKD/CBD:** Certified Kitchen Designer/ Certified Bath Designer	**APLD:** Association of Professional Landscape Designers **Horticulture** **Garden Centers**

sign. It requires work experience and passing an exam.

The letters CSI stand for Construction Specifiers Institute. Any professional members in good standing may use the designation CSI after their name. CSI offers the following certification programs:

CDT: Construction Document Technologist

CCCA: Certified Construction Contract Administrator

CCS: Certified Construction Specifier

CCPR: Certified Construction Product Representative

The letters LEED stand for Leadership in Energy and Environmental Design. The LEED program is a certification program. LEED certifies buildings and industry individuals for their knowledge of LEED practices. The letters LEED AP stand for Leadership in Energy and Environmental Design Accredited Professional. The LEED professional credentials are professional designations for those who have demonstrated a thorough understanding of green building techniques, environmental issues, the LEED program, and the certification process. LEED offers the following certifications:

LEED Green Associate

LEED AP BD+C: Building Design and Construction

LEED AP ID+C: Interior Design and Construction

LEED AP O+M: Building Operations and Maintenance

LEED AP ND: Neighborhood Development

LEED AP: Homes

The letters NKBA stand for National Kitchen and Bath Association. NKBA-certified designers demonstrate comprehensive knowledge in kitchen and bath design, as well as construction, mechanical, plumbing, and electrical systems. The NKBA certifies kitchen and bath professionals in various levels of expertise and provides two distinct paths, one for the kitchen and bath designers, and one for non-design professionals. The NKBA offers the following certifications:

AKBD: Associate Kitchen and Bath Designer

CKD/CBD: Certified Kitchen Designer/ Certified Bath Designer

CKE/CBE: Certified Kitchen Educators/ Certified Bath Educators

CMKBD: Certified Master Kitchen and Bath Designer

CMKBE: Certified Master Kitchen and Bath Educator

CKBP: Certified Kitchen and Bath Professional

"With an architect as your guide, you can responsibly stop worrying about what spaces someone else might want in a house and focus only on those things your house should include."

➢ *Targeted expenditures:* An architect can design a home to maximize "bang for the buck." This is accomplished through creatively planning higher spatial utility, and constructing only and exactly what you want and are likely to use. Extra rooms you never use, along with endless hallways, are left on the cutting room floor and never make it into your floor plans. With an architect as your guide, you can responsibly stop worrying about what spaces someone else might want in a house and focus only on those things your house should include. The resultant savings in eliminating unwanted and unused areas will reduce the amount of construction, freeing up those resources to be applied elsewhere.

➢ *Higher value:* Studies show that good design commands a price premium that can often offset the initial added cost for the design. When you use an architect, your costs are limited to those of actual construction, plus design fees. Where the appraised value of your home exceeds the cost plus design fees, the differential, or value created by design, adds to your bottom line and equity position. This financial dividend can prove significant over time as it is leveraged on what is likely your largest investment.

➤ *Streamlined process:* An architect knows the hierarchy of decision making, and can guide choices of elements and variables. Design skills are applied toward streamlining a process that extends beyond setting dates for selecting fixtures and finishes and helps manage your entire team, decisions, communications, and expectations from initial sketches to final completion.

➤ *Construction oversight:* Your architect can serve as your agent during construction, administer your construction contract, and keep you involved and informed of the progress and upcoming decisions. Your architect can answer questions from your contractor and suppliers, define and confirm acceptable levels of quality, and reject nonconforming work. Who better to insure that construction actually follows the design documents than the professional who prepared those documents? An architect is licensed to watch over the details of the drawings and construction and to enforce your agreement with a contractor to provide the results you expect.

➤ *Applied building science and technology:* An architect has an up-to-date working knowledge of building science and technology and is equipped to advise you on your selections of materials, fixtures, appliances, finishes, and systems. Buildings look simple, but what makes them function and hold together is frequently hidden from view. They are quite complex and prone to rapid decay unless the design and detail issues are resolved before construction.

➤ *Costly mistake prevention:* Misunderstanding how materials or assemblies perform and interact with each other before they are installed can become expensive lessons, especially when something must be replaced, repaired, or continually repainted. Seemingly small or

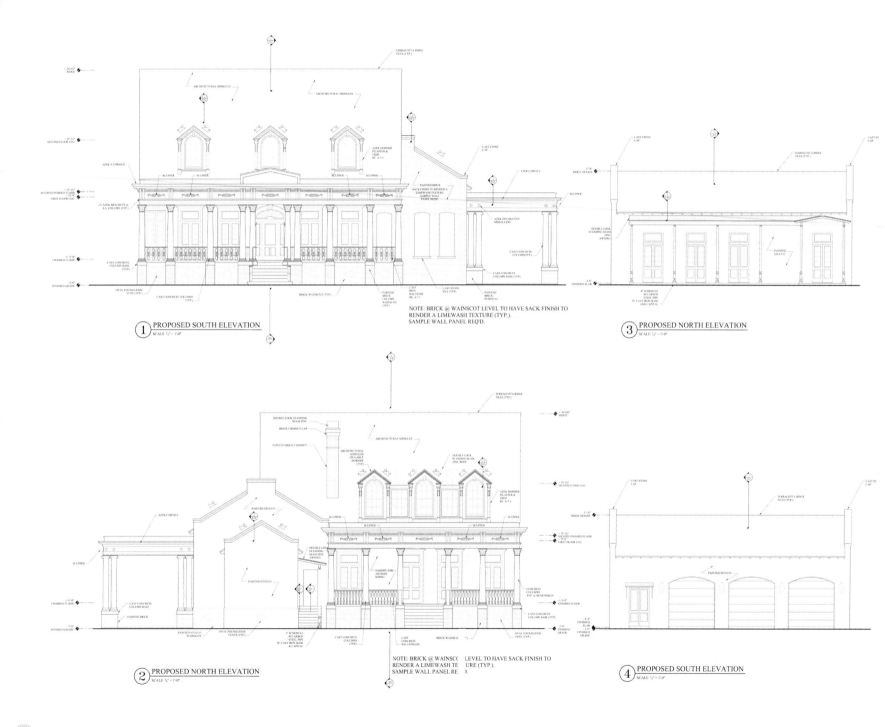

① PROPOSED SOUTH ELEVATION
SCALE ⅛" = 1'-0"

③ PROPOSED NORTH ELEVATION
SCALE ⅛" = 1'-0"

NOTE: BRICK @ WAINSCOT LEVEL TO HAVE SACK FINISH TO
RENDER A LIMEWASH TEXTURE (TYP.).
SAMPLE WALL PANEL REQ'D.

② PROPOSED NORTH ELEVATION
SCALE ⅛" = 1'-0"

NOTE: BRICK @ WAINSCOT LEVEL TO HAVE SACK FINISH TO
RENDER A LIMEWASH TEXTURE (TYP.).
SAMPLE WALL PANEL REQ'D.

④ PROPOSED SOUTH ELEVATION
SCALE ⅛" = 1'-0"

40

insignificant selections, such as flashing for a window, hardware for kitchen cabinets, or materials for an exterior door, can all become costly mistakes. An architect can guide you through your selections and decisions, advise about problems likely to result, and provide you with creative alternatives that will still achieve your intentions.

➢ *Aesthetic sensibility:* An architect's aesthetic sensibility includes knowing the "intent" of design elements that allow appropriate and authentic use of a wide variety of details. It is common to see rows of subdivision houses trying to mimic good design, predefining the elements of a style but randomly applying ornamental features such as columns, brackets, crown molding, window trims, and so on. Utilizing architectural details without any clear understanding of why they were created and how they were originally applied can end up with a "Mr. Potato Head" result to house design. Someone takes a handful of elements and, basically, sticks them on a house, much as a baby might attach the parts to the Potato Head toy. In both situations the correct parts may get used, just not in an appropriate context. This often produces an inharmonious result in which the "vibe" is "off" or just not quite right. This disconnection of the parts from the whole can be humorous on a toy but unfortunate on a house.

➢ *Healthy and inspirational spaces:* Much of the architect's education focuses on making environments both healthful and enjoyable, from the technical aspects of insuring air and light quality to the artistic notions of assembling materials and spaces that celebrate the human spirit. When using an architect, this broad range of expertise, from technical awareness (health) to artful intention (inspiration), becomes a valuable asset. A home designed by a talented, experienced architect in tune with your personality, lifestyle, culture, climate, and budget will likely become a cherished heirloom to be passed down through generations. Such a forever home has the intangible power to capture the spirit and essence of what it means to be you.

➤ *Psychological dividends:* Persuading materials and humans to cooperate with any set of predefined intentions, budgets, and schedules can be a daunting and stressful task. During the challenges associated with both design and construction, engaging a design professional can provide you with peace of mind. An experienced architect can help you more safely navigate the process, steer clear of troublesome obstacles, and safeguard your positive experience throughout the process.

➤ *Increased visibility:* The appearance of order is fundamental to any work of architecture and delights us when the results are beautiful. A home balanced in geometry and proportion will inevitably be set apart from its surroundings, become more noticed, and referenced with pride by any family and in any community.

➤ *Positive effect on surrounding property:* Your neighbors will also benefit from your good design. Developers have long known the positive effect that good architecture influences on surrounding properties and this is often used as a catalyst for economic development. The first homes built in a subdivision set the tone for the quality expected and relative value of what will follow. Likewise, when well-designed homes appear in sufficient number in an existing neighborhood, they establish a positive trend for future renovations and an increase in property values.

What Should I Expect if I Decide to "Go It Alone?"

That is a fair question, and my answer is based upon what I have gathered from clients sharing their experiences from prior ventures into design and construction. Both design and construction are complex problems with countless variables. Many of these options are intertwined in an intricate lacework of consequences not immediately apparent to the novice. Every homeowner "going it alone" will learn a great deal about the design and construction of a home. These learning curves are steep and can become expensive lessons when subject mastery lags behind construction progress. Many homeowners find

"Should you decide to 'go it alone,' the sections of this book on knowing yourself, creating a team, and the construction process will give you some foundational knowledge for an optimal decision."

the details of design and construction an unfamiliar territory and become overwhelmed by the complexities of the process. Inexperience comes with lack of insight, which leads to stress, poor choices, and changes that negatively affect the construction cost, time required for completion, and the homebuilding experience.

Should you decide to "go it alone," the sections of this book on knowing yourself, creating a team, and the construction process will give you some foundational knowledge for an optimal decision. Good design is not about selecting only the very best, or simply using cost as the deciding factor. Rather, it is more about the selective editing through what is appropriate for the situation and balancing the many factors of cost, time for procurement and construction, efficiency of resources, functionality, operating costs, maintenance costs, building codes, and of course, aesthetics.

How Architects Charge

Architects use three basic methods to determine their fees: hourly plus expenses, a percentage of the construction costs, or a flat fee. There can be variations and combinations as well. Each usually includes a provision for additional amounts should you request changes to the drawings or to the construction later in the process.

➤ *Hourly:* Rates vary by experience and reputation and can go as low as $50 per hour for architects just getting started to well above $200 per hour for seasoned professionals who bring to the table more experience and a proven reputation for excellence. While a younger architect may possess exceptional talent, architecture is a profession with a continually steep learning curve. In many ways, there is so much to learn about history, building construction, and people, that architecture often appears to be a profession of late bloomers. Hence, higher fees are justified for projects that can tap into the wisdom learned from experience.

➤ *Percentages:* Fees based on percentages of the construction costs vary by the level of services expected from the architect and can range from as low as 6 percent to more than 25 percent. For a full-service fee, engaging an architect from conception through construction, expect the fees to range beyond 12 percent. I recommend getting clarity on the level of involvement offered by your architect throughout construction for any project, but especially when proposed fees are on the lower side of 6 to 10 percent.

To make an informed decision, do not assume that a lower quoted percentage is a bargain, or that a higher fee ensures better work. Look for equivalents. For example, say you get a quote from one architect for 6 percent and another for 12 percent. Is the 6 percent fee the bargain? Not necessarily. Everyone in the business must make a profit to stay in business. So whatever fee is negotiated will translate into a fixed amount of time and scope of services. In order for firms to charge on the lowest end of the scale, certain accommodations will need to be made to make that fee financially feasible. If not, and there is a misunderstanding on the architect's part about the time required, he or she will learn a quick and expensive lesson and end up with a dissatisfied client or both. A reduced fee can be achieved by limiting the number of hours spent on your project. It could mean cloning or recycling previous designs and discouraging customization. Architects who promote a particular or signature style have the ability to use each subsequent house design as a "laboratory" to test and perfect their ideas. This can be desirable when you want that particular style.

A lower fee may mask the true cost by eliminating key components included in a higher fee, such as mechanical and electrical drawings. If you have to pay out of pocket for these to get your building permit, you may actually end up paying close to the same amount you would have paid if you had opted for the higher fee. A lower fee may be appropriate when the owner is willing to make concessions in terms of scope, time, cost, or quality in order to justify the reduced fee. Likewise, if you are investing on the upper end of the scale, what additional services, experience, or other benefits are you getting in return for that investment?

How to Find and Select the Architect for You

Custom residential architecture is a reputation-driven business. As such, the best way to identify potential candidates for your forever home would be to check with friends, neighbors, and acquaintances who have had their own experiences with an architect. Another method is to contact the American Institute of Architects (AIA) and request a list of architects in your area who include custom residential design in their practice. The AIA has state and local chapters throughout the United States.

Most of my clients come from past clients' recommendations. In the past few years, an increasing number of clients located me by searching the Internet, viewing images of my work, and then calling to set up an interview.

Regardless of how you develop your list of architects, the final selection should be based upon an interview. Engaging an architect, especially one you will entrust with the challenge of designing your forever home, should be a process of mutual selection. You, of course, must be comfortable with your selection and your architect must be comfortable with the prospect of working with you to achieve the home of your dreams. The feeling must be mutual. I've found that scheduling a free, one-hour meeting with potential clients is the best way for us to get to know each other. After an hour is spent talking about the home my clients envision and the design process I use, we can each get an idea of whether or not it's a good fit.

WHAT TO LOOK FOR

Review the qualifications and experience of the individual with whom you will be working throughout this one- to three-year process. Confirm his or her propensity to listen to your needs and interests, and to check on your feelings, such that you can trust this individual to always have your best interests at heart. Obtain a list of references and contact them to confirm any interview observations and/or hesitations. In the end, feeling comfortable with whom you select is

Specific Questions to Ask

1. Have the professionals you are considering hiring designed many custom homes similar in size and complexity to what you have in mind?

2. Do they have a preferred style, or is each house unique?

3. What is their process and how involved will you be in the decision making?

4. What is their current backlog of work and when can they start your project?

5. Are they members of any professional organizations?

6. Are they active in any professional groups related to custom residential design?

7. Have they had their work published? Have they received any design awards?

8. How do they charge for their services?

9. What is the range of expected construction costs based on their experience of similar projects?

the most important consideration of all. From that all else will flow.

The Owner/Architect Contract

Once you decide on an architect, I advise using a contract that defines the expectations and duties of both you and your architect and details the fee arrangement. Other contracts are readily available, but I strongly recommend using AIA contracts. The AIA has been offering consensus-based documents to the construction industry for over 150 years, and they are broadly accepted as an industry standard. I also recommend using an equivalent AIA contract with your contractor. Ask your architect about using the AIA documents developed especially for custom residential projects to guide all of your construction agreements. The use of paired owner-architect and owner-contractor contracts coordinates, in a consistent legal language, the contractual duties and project expectations of you, your architect, and your contractor.

Being happy in your own home can be as simple as including a peaceful area to collect your thoughts or sip your coffee.

CHAPTER TWO

There's No House without "U" (You)

"It's a helluva start, being able to recognize what makes you happy."

—LUCILLE BALL

Know Thyself

Inscribed on the ancient Greek Temple of Apollo at Delphi is the concise statement *Gnothi seauton*, which translates as "Know thyself." This original advice was, and is still, the best possible place to start any serious journey. It is also where you should begin exploring designs for something as important as your home. Residential architecture houses the most intimate of life's activities, and throughout the process you will learn much about yourself, your likes, dislikes, and limits.

As you begin, it is important to pause and examine yourself and your family. Your combined backgrounds, travels, personality, and inclinations will influence your decisions. Spend time identifying your preferences and compare these features with whatever is lacking in your current living quarters. Don't worry about dreaming of features or results that may prove to be more sizzle than steak. Throughout the design process, you and your architect will explore these imagined options to determine their potential to resonate with your lifestyle and budget.

Ten Areas to Explore

These 10 areas are a good place to start the discernment process. Keep in mind that there are no right or wrong answers. The following questions, and your answers, are neutral, but will help you to identify the right fit of options in meaningful terms for your architect or designer.

An open plan provides a multifunction space conducive to a variety of family activities.

1. FUNCTIONS

What activities (functions) do you want to take place in your home? Do you entertain often? Do you want to but can't in your present surroundings? Do you like to cook or do you have a home-based hobby? Do you spend most of your time indoors or outdoors? Do you prefer formal or casual dining? How do you relax at the end of the day? Identifying these and other functions your house should accommodate will help define the basic problems the design solution must address.

2. YOUR BACKGROUND, LIFESTYLE, AND EXPERIENCE

Where did you grow up? Was it in one place, or did your family travel? Describe a handful of memories from your home and family life. What aspects did you like? What would you change in your next house? What is your current lifestyle? Describe a typical weekday, weekend, and holiday activity. How and how often do you entertain family and friends?

3. IS THERE A SHARED VISION (HUSBAND/WIFE/PARTNERS)?

Do you and your partner have a shared vision in terms of space, function, and look? If not, what are each individual's goals for the project? I'm often asked how my process resolves the design when couples do not have the same vision. Provided these are design differences and not veiled relationship issues, creative joy comes from discovering areas to express individual contrasts and common grounds. This cross-fertilization often results in an artistic fusion that is a unique blend of both partners, not unlike mixing separate chromosomes to form a new whole. One of the most interesting, and artistically challenging, aspects of residential design is the process of mixing this "design DNA."

4. "GREEN" CONCERNS

What is your level of concern with the environmental impact of your construction? Are you willing to invest more resources for a future return and savings to the environment?

Central to this issue of "green" is the idea of ecosystem sustainability: making smart decisions to reduce potentially harmful effects from construction and life cycle operations. Proponents advocate lessening energy consumption for construction while minimizing the depletion of nonrenewable resources. Reducing materials transportation costs through utilizing local materials is not a new concept, nor is the idea of a building that requires minimal energy for its ongoing operation. The effectiveness of any civilization has shown to be related to its utilization of local materials, labor, and the wise conservation of natural resources.

Vernacular houses designed for each region were the original "green" buildings. They were crafted to be responsive to the environment, available materials, and respecting site conditions. But what about all of the new construction products? Does your house have to ignore the past in order to take advantage of technological improvements? Any common-sense design approach readily incorporates problem-solving inventions and new materials, especially when reducing resource consumption and maintenance in ways not before possible, or to increase occupant comfort. For example, wood shingles have been replaced by lower-maintenance and longer-lasting roofing systems, and the thermal comfort provided by high ceilings and operable windows in southern Louisiana can be satisfied through building insulation and mechanical air conditioning.

While I support green concerns and sustainability, I caution all homeowners to be aware of products simply labeled green that may, in reality, cost more than they promise to save. I have found that the tried and true principals that guided traditional design most often satisfy the overarching goals of the green movement more than many exotic "green" offerings.

Rustic bricks reassembled beneath majestic salvaged beams honor the hand wrought labor of unknown ancestors. This memory is juxtaposed by master craftsmen against the polished finishes of upholstered furniture, center-match beaded siding and plaster ceilings.

Timeless design, I believe, is the ultimate in sustainability.

5. FOREVER HOME OR "FOR NOW" HOME

Is this a home you plan to live in forever? Or do you plan to live in it "for now?" No one can predict the future, but knowing how long you plan to live in your new home should figure into its design and budget.

For example, when my wife and I bought our third home, situated one block from the high school all three of our girls would attend, we were willing to invest more in the renovation. We anticipated at least a 10-year horizon, the time before the youngest would graduate. So we designed the home for function and comfort and to be as fine as we could afford. Given our plans to reside there for a full decade, it seemed reasonable to increase our budget. That proved to

An elegant stair, treads gently curving, spills into the foyer in a welcoming puddle- an iconic feature in stately Southern homes. This gracious foyer welcomes family and guests, playing center stage for the family's most treasured events. Memories of being wrapped in holiday decor or ornamented with children descending in prom dresses or wedding attire, add to their charm.

be a very wise decision. It gave us a convenient location in a neighborhood where appreciated values enhanced our initial investment. Had this been our starter home and in a fringe neighborhood, we would not have pushed our financial envelope.

6. LIFE STAGE: DESIRE TO "GRACE IN PLACE"

Are you fresh out of school or a young couple? Expecting children? Are you part of the sandwich generation, a three-generation household of you, your children, and aging parents?

Your stage in life and what you can expect in the foreseeable future should impact your design decisions. Future needs at odds with your current budget could benefit from a master plan that defines your house project in phases. In this way, what is included in the initial construction phase would meet your current needs and be able to accept prearranged future additions with minimal expense and disruption.

There is a growing trend for people to remain in their home for as long as possible as they age. Consider design features that support this goal. *Grace in place* is the phrase I use to embody my attitude toward aging in place, ADA accessibility, and universal design. This requires designing to fit for today as well as for the twilight years. Your home would gracefully accommodate elderly movement throughout with wider halls and doorways. Make them wide enough for a walker or wheelchair, and whenever possible, avoid split-level floor plans. One attractive result from a house with sunken rooms is the interest and room separation higher (or lower) ceilings provide. I recommend achieving these gains through modulating the ceilings and not the floors, as it is, ultimately, safer and does not compromise accessibility.

Many features that support aging in place have little influence on initial construction budgets. However, their absence eliminates use by anyone with physical challenges. Imagine recovering from surgery or

This alternative to an open plan uses pocket doors to connect the family room to the adjacent kitchen. Open French doors extend the living space to the outdoor entertainment veranda.

> "Without professional guidance, it is easy to fall into the trap of trying to become an expert, considering far too many options, and experiencing a form of decision paralysis that is maddening to everyone involved."

a broken foot while living in a home with features that such an injury would make difficult or impossible to access. Completing mundane tasks, such as taking a bath or using the kitchen, become difficult endeavors. The rewards for having a user-friendly home, for whenever you need, justifies planning ahead.

7. TOLERANCE

By tolerance, I mean your patience for making innumerable decisions, selections, and resolving conflicts. An architect can guide you through all of the decisions, using professional judgment to limit the choices presented and simplify the process. There are hundreds of selections to make. Some are important and require careful consideration; some only require an educated guess. Without professional guidance, it is easy to fall into the trap of trying to become an expert, considering far too many options, and experiencing a form of decision paralysis that is maddening to everyone involved.

In addition to the issue of making selections, every construction project is a breeding ground for conflicts. Each clash comes with the potential to affect construction due to misunderstanding expectations, inattention to details, or botched attempts to cut a corner or two.

Again, your architect is available to help manage these issues. Use your design team to manage the commotion and make building a house a delightful experience.

8. INVESTMENT

I recommend that you define up front what you are willing, or able, to invest in your project. Include approximately 10 percent extra as a buffer for any surprises and minor enhancements you may add after construction has commenced. Share these amounts with your architect at the beginning. Also, share how you plan to access your resources. If you involve a lending institution, it is important that your architect is familiar with that institution's required approvals, schedules, and ongoing paperwork during construction and through completion.

9. ASPIRATIONS AND EMOTIONS

What do you hope to accomplish by building or remodeling? Will it be an expression of your uniqueness? Is it to be designed for the site and to maximize some amaz-ing views? Will it be the go-to home for social functions and hosting parties for the grandchildren? Is it to be a cozy cottage for two where you can live easily, quietly, and efficiently? Identifying your aspirations is fundamental to the design of your forever home.

10. SENSITIVITY TO DESIGN

Get to the heart of your individual "design sensitivity." How important is design to you and why? Do you have any aesthetic concerns you want addressed with your project? Are there any particular homes that have caught your eye? Good design is fashionable. Great design is timeless.

The Style File

This part of the process begins with your creating a style file of photos and short notes conveying features you like about each image or idea. The concept is to design your home to capture that feeling shown in the photographs by being honestly influenced by the imag-

Windows and French doors visually enlarge a room.

room, kitchen, living room, and so on. I use the term *at-mosphere* to mean the feeling a particular room should convey. Words alone cannot adequately describe *atmosphere*, and photographs are usually burdened with unwanted materials, details, colors, or furniture. However, by notating these photographs with edited descriptions of specific features or characteristics my clients desire, I will be able to identify useful fragments to incorporate into the detailed design. For example, photos of a historical library may have an "air" my clients want to incorporate into their den, or the design of a magnificent staircase might influence features in their foyer. Photos that capture some aesthetic aspect help guide the design. The result is a combination of materials, lighting, and architectural elements that will most likely resonate with my clients' tastes.

es and not simply by the contents. Replication is rarely required. The final design should capture the spirit of these rooms through fresh translations and incorporate details unique to your home.

Once my clients and I have identified all of the functions, size, and arrangement of spaces and they have been placed on a floor plan, I must understand what mood or "atmospheres" my clients prefer for their bed-

VISUAL VOCABULARY

I prefer the visual language of photographs because words are woefully inadequate for describing style.

What one person sees as preferable is not always a universal truth. Through a photographic style file you can confirm that both you and your architect are speaking the same visual language.

These images don't have to be elaborate and can take many different forms, but what each has in common is helping the designer understand, on an emotional and artistic level, what home owners want for their home. When I look at the photos and read the comments, I will absorb your likes and dislikes, and I will learn which colors and shapes make you comfortable. They inform a visual vocabulary to describe your home.

REALITY CHECK

The style process can also serve as a reality check. For example, you may wish to only spend $40,000 on a kitchen remodel but assemble a style file full of high-end appliances such as a Wolf range or exquisite fixtures from Waterworks. I recommend these brands as excellent choices but must emphasize that there is an inescapable price premium associated with fine items and materials. Before serious design work can go any further, I suggest talking about the impending need to either adjust the budget in order to include those expensive features, or revisit some of the selections. The best time for adjusting expectations is early in the process.

WHAT CAN A STYLE FILE LOOK LIKE?

One of my early clients taught me, by example, how to beautifully create and organize a notebook filled with photos from magazines, and notes on each image about what she liked. She poured enormous energy into this style file over the years and the end result genuinely helped my understanding of the goals the final design was to achieve. It is rare for a client to invest so much time in assembling a style file.

More common is the client with stacks of books and magazines laced with sticky notes.

Today, however, digital apps afford free access to literally millions of images of what others in the digital ethos have done. These now help clients assemble and share their atmosphere photos.

Whatever method you use, don't overthink it. Don't overwhelm yourself by choosing every light fixture and faucet. Instead, focus on editing your selections to only contain images that truly speak to you.

YOUR HOME'S STORY

Every house tells a story, and designing one allows you to write the script. I ask my clients for clues they want to display, and what they want their house to say to present-day "archaeologists" passing by or visiting. New, as well as ancient or historic structures, serve as three-dimensional textbooks, revealing stories that depict a culture's values and way of life. What story will your home tell?

HOW DOES AN ARCHITECT USE YOUR STYLE FILE?

Going through a style file is a completely right-brain activity. As I sort through each image, I pose clarifying questions. But more often than not, I'm completely silent. It may appear that nothing's going on, but my brain is working at full speed, taking in nonverbal clues and forming impressions. By the time I've finished absorbing the content of the file, I've developed a strong sense of your individual style, including the mood and feelings you'd like in your home. I am then ready to begin designing the third dimension of elevations and sections and exploring your resulting style.

Know Thy Property

Knowing yourself also extends to knowing your property. Whether you decide to go it alone, hire an architect, or something in between, the following items will form the foundation of the design work. Gather them early.

➢ *Site plan or survey:* This document, prepared by a surveyor, locates an existing house on the prop-

Renovations to this 1930s cottage accommodate today's lifestyles. A salvaged timber beam replaces the old dividing wall to join family and kitchen areas.

erty. It also indicates lot lines, utility connections, flood plain status, zoning classification, and servitudes. It is often included with your closing documents.

➢ *Subdivision restrictions (if applicable):* Many subdivisions limit what can be built with covenants more restrictive than the county or city building requirements. These covenants can limit the materials, establish mandatory building setbacks, and require approval of building and landscape. Look in your closing documents for these. If you aren't sure if your subdivision has such restrictions, check with your real estate agent, closing attorney, or neighborhood association.

➢ *Floor plans (for renovations):* A copy of your home's plans is the best record, although the drawings from many older homes have long since been discarded or lost. If original plans are unavailable, check your closing documents for a simple plan that may have been included in the appraisal or in the description of the property.

➢ *Photographs of the exterior (for renovations):* It is always good to have a photographic record of before images of both the interior as well as the exterior. Take photos of the front, sides, and rear of your home.

This façade leaves no doubt about where to knock.

CHAPTER THREE

An Architect-Led Design Process

"Things which matter most must never be at the mercy of things which matter least."

—Johann Wolfgang von Goethe

Understanding the "Hierarchy of Design"

I've come to realize that designing a home doesn't begin with determining which style you want. In fact, no matter where you plan to build or what kind of home you envision, its authentic style is the conclusive result of many factors, and it only develops toward the end of the design process, not at its beginning. In other words, don't let the conclusion "tail" end up wagging the bigger body of decisions (the "dog") and jeopardizing your success. There is a natural hierarchy in which certain decisions must be made, and the best results occur when they are addressed in their proper order. Make the big decisions, the choices that will be hard if not impossible to change later, before focusing on the smaller decisions that can readily change without causing a major alteration. Just as a pilot first takes a view from 5,000 feet and then glides lower, makes subtle adjustments, and flies even lower, making finer adjustments as he nears the runway, so I approach design projects by first taking in the big picture and gradually zeroing in on the details in iterative passes.

I refer to this process as the *hierarchy of design*. It is a sequence that begins with the neighborhood (the big picture) and then drops lower and lower to focus on the lot, floor plan, style, and stylistic details. In this way, decisions that are typically harder, if not impossible, to change later in the process, are soundly determined before switching your focus to more detailed and independently adjustable decisions. For example, too often home owners will select a floor plan independent of, and before choosing, their parcel, and they discover too late that the great exterior views are impossible when the afternoon sun overpowers the living room, or that their perfect master bathroom is open to view from the neighbors' living room. These and many other issues presented by the site selected are discoverable early in the process and should influence the floor plan. This is because your floor plan is more easily adjustable than is your neighbor's house, or the predictable path of the sun.

STEP 1: THE NEIGHBORHOOD

The biggest decision when building or renovating is to select the area or neighborhood. I cannot overemphasize the importance of choosing a location that appeals to you and your lifestyle before you invest much time on less important matters. Why? Because no matter how fine a house I design, one single home is too small to change the character of an entire neighborhood. Realtors will confirm the economic wisdom of choosing a neighborhood of homes with a similar value to what you plan to build. I add to this advice the reminder that it's important to choose a convenient neighborhood: one that's close to work, school, and basic shopping. If possible, you want to be able to enjoy the sanctuary of your home instead of spending more of your day commuting.

A neighborhood's character and value is determined by reviewing the surrounding properties and calculating an average. One exception to this rule is the isolated estate lot, where a single home is the defining element. The second exception is choosing a neighborhood where the surrounding properties do not define the character, as they are destined for imminent renovation or demolition. Be cautious however, if your plan is to buy a home in a neighborhood currently wanting. Ultimate success with future outcomes depends upon your accurately predicting market reactions and further enhancements to adja-

Curved landing and handrails provide a grand stairway without overpowering the foyer.

cent properties. This level of prediction is, at best, a dicey proposition.

Unless your forever-home ideal will be located on a visually remote estate lot, my recommendation is to select your neighborhood based on the following considerations:

> *Existing friendship network*: Where does your social group of friends live? Will you, or your kids, need to build a new set of friends?

> *Quality of life features:* How is the physical health of the neighborhood? Are there nearby parks and playgrounds, sidewalks, jogging paths, bike trails, golf courses, or lakes?

> *School district:* Is the neighborhood in a desirable school district, or will locating there necessitate private schools for your children?

> *Convenience:* It is important to choose a neighborhood that's easily accessible to work, schools, and basic shopping. You want to be able to enjoy the sanctuary of your home without spending much of the day in your car. Will day-to-day trips involve congestion and traffic? Are the routes to and from the location scenic and beautiful? Are there public commuting options?

> *Groceries and restaurants:* Are there convenient grocery stores, a nearby farmer's market, or neighborhood restaurants?

> *Neighborhood metrics:* Is the value in the neighborhood stable? What are recent home sales price increases? How long does it take homes to sell, on average? What is the current inventory of homes for sale? Are public areas clean and adequately maintained? Are the homes also neat and well kept?

This home employs the architectural device of axis to organize the spaces, flow, and experience. Alignment of arches, vaulted ceilings, and openings make the house live bigger than its square footage.

> "The parcel you choose will end up influencing your home's design, whether you're renovating an existing house or building from scratch."

STEP 2: THE LOT

After you've found a neighborhood that's right for you, its time to select a specific lot from the available properties. The parcel you choose will end up influencing your home's design, whether you're renovating an existing house or building from scratch. For example, I always consider privacy issues when sketching floor plans. Factoring in visual privacy without sacrificing daylight and outside views is an important part of my design process. I've witnessed far too many gorgeous master bedrooms that, due to a lack of visual privacy, prompted homeowners to install heavy blackout curtains that convert well-lit rooms into upholstered caves. And that's a shame since outdoor views and natural lighting are psychologically important, providing openness and a sense of connection to your surroundings. Other lot considerations that influence design include the direction of sunlight, views of adjacent structures and mature trees, soil conditions, drainage, and whether electricity, cable, and telephone lines are above or below ground. The shape of your lot is less important than other factors, as I've found that the challenge of building on an oddly shaped property often results in a home with a most interesting and pleasing geometry.

STEP 3: THE FLOOR PLAN

After selecting a neighborhood and a lot, I turn the attention to your family's lifestyle. My goal is to design a floor plan that fits you like a custom suit of clothes, which locates the fabric only where it is needed and trims, or edits, where it is not. For example, when designing a home for an active family with kids involved in sports, I'll include, by the garage entrance, an area dedicated as a "drop zone" where the kids can stash their gear in individual lockers. I think carefully about what each room in your house needs to accommodate and how the rooms flow together within zones, both inside and outside. I also consider the experience that guests have as they approach the house, as well as the functionality of the floor plan when you host larger groups. The end result is a livable and accommodating space for your family's everyday use, as well as for entertaining.

STEP 4: THE FINAL TOUCH

I believe true style is the result of a whole series of influences and should only be determined at the end of the process. Determining an authentic look that is appropriate for your forever home comes as a conclusive flourish

A projecting balcony provides welcoming cover to a West Indies-influenced courtyard entry.

Gently curved stairs and balcony create a delightful piano nook and a gracious entry hall.

of style. Since style is influenced by your likes and dislikes, I spend time discussing and absorbing your style file. This is where I zero in and fine-tune the details: Do you like a light and airy feeling? Wood beams? Hard materials such as stone? Warm or cool colors? After I've developed a strong sense of your individual style, I explore how these elements would contribute and enhance the design, dressing your home in a way that's unique to you, reflects your style preferences, possesses a comfortable functionality, and is perfectly suited to your neighborhood, lot, and family.

My Design Process

Looking back at how I designed homes over the decades, I realized that I was instinctively repeating an identifiable process that guided how I "intuitively" approached each project. Committing these major steps to paper allowed me to better communicate expectations to my staff while providing clients with a road map of expectations along the way. Knowing the big-pic-

I   **II**   **III**   **IV**   **Phase**

ture process helps everyone involved to sequence and batch decision energy where it best aids the entire effort. I share this overview of my design process to help clients orchestrate their decisions in concert with the project team.

My process, as illustrated above, begins with signing the owner-architect contract for your forever home. I immediately begin defining the goals for your house. I visit the site, explore its unique characteristics and potential, and identify any additional information that may be required, such as property and topographic surveys, specific locations of specimen trees, including their drip

lines, or a soils report to guide the design of a solid foundation.

While collecting and refining the above programmatic information, I prepare a series of drawings, in multiple iterations of presentation-review and revision. These schematic design schemes start with solving the mostly two-dimensional room function and site relationships. By "two-dimensional," I mean looking at your site and floor plan for length and width dimensions, such as setbacks; servitudes; room sizes; flow from one adjacent space to another; convenient and accessible locations of key functions; kitchen arrangement and work triangle; and universal access features including width of hallways, door openings, and level changes.

After the two-dimensional layout appears resolved, introducing the third dimension of walls and rooflines visually tests these arrangements for a pleasing composition. The third dimension incorporates elevation views, room volume, façade arrangement, roof shapes, and the sculptural massing of the entire house. In this iteration, window and door locations are checked against how they affect the overall configuration and are adjusted as necessary.

The schematic process concludes with a set of scaled drawings that illustrate how your floor plan will be laid out, what size each room needs to be to accommodate its function, and how everything will look when built.

Fine detailing and further development of this design will then come to a temporary halt until we have the contributions of your contractor, as well as any additional design team members (interior designer, landscape architect, etc.).

I find the greatest planning success occurs when the entire team collaborates before any final detailed drawings are prepared. I meet jointly with the contractor and each of the major subcontractors to troubleshoot the schematic design for any issues they might anticipate. The final drawings are prepared with the full benefit of this involvement prior to final pricing or directing of the construction.

I also review the schematic designs to share criticisms and creative ideas with the full design team. This involves everyone on the design team including you, the interior designer, the landscape architect, and me. It is critical that we are all on the same conceptual page. I call this portion of the process design development. Following these development meetings, the final drawings are prepared, detailing a proposal that is true to your intent and purpose and tempered by the multiple points of view of construction, interiors, and landscaping.

Preparing a detailed set of coordinated drawings is very time consuming, and to assure you that I am on track with your desires, I share our partial drawings with you, your construction team, and your design team for feedback at 50 percent, 75 percent, and 100 percent points of completion.

Once completed, I present you with a set of final drawings for one last review and approval. After I receive your approval, I release the drawings for final pricing and construction.

The contractor assembles final bids, which can take from two to four weeks. I then review the detailed

Inspired by structures over plantation water wells, this rustic portico welcomes familiar guests into a quiet garden outside the side entryway.

French doors lead out the side of the home to the porte cochere, a covered drive-through that offers protection from inclement weather.

costing with both you and the contractor. Adjustments necessary to the scope of work are identified, priced, and approved by you before I prepare a contract between you and your contractor. I prefer to be involved through construction, actively observing progress, comparing what is built with what was drawn, and serving as the communication conduit during construction. See Chapter 5 for more information on my recommended construction process.

Other Design Processes

Design-Bid-Build and Design-Build are alternative design and construction delivery methods. They differ from my approach in two important ways: when and how you engage with the contractor. My process combines what I believe are the positive attributes of each into a workable hybrid.

DESIGN-BID-BUILD

The oldest approach to design and construction is to (1) design what you want, (2) solicit bids from multiple contractors, (3) select one, and (4) begin construction. The logic of this approach is to separate the designer from the contractor to avoid conflicts of interest and maintain a design purity uninfluenced by anticipated difficulty or profit, all while obtaining the best price for the work through competitive bidding between contractors.

DESIGN-BUILD

The more recent approach of design-build advocates combining the responsibilities of design and construction into a single entity and requires the owner to sign a single contract for both design and construction. The biggest advantages of this method come from the in-house connecting of the designer's knowledge and experience with those of the craftsmen. More accurate early estimates are possible, with fewer drawings required to communicate design intent from conception to construction. Both design and construction activities are managed by a single concern. This method has been shown to reduce construction time and cost on many projects and has been both sanctioned (as an ethical approach) and promoted (as a practice option) by the AIA.

A growing number of architects now offer the design-build option and serve also as the contractor for their designs. All responsibility and liability are with one company, with a single contract. Many states now recognize contracts that engage a single entity for both design and construction responsibilities.

COMPARISON

The design-bid-build approach engages the contractor after final drawings have been prepared and produces the lowest price for the work described in the drawings. Design-build engages the contractor simultaneously with the designer and can promise to save both time

A Studio Soundboard full of dials, slides, and buttons used to set, adjust, and confirm the variables such as musical pitch, tone, timing, etc., from multiple soundtracks, to finally produce a single composition.
(Photo credit: Wikimedia Commons.)

and costs. Both, on their surface, have advantages. So why do I not use either one?

I started my practice using the design-bid-build process and soon experienced disappointment with the approach. Relying upon information from cost-estimating manuals as a guide, I found they did not provide the ac-

curate pricing needed for preliminary selections or decision making. This resulted in client decisions based on an optimism unfiltered by the reality of actual costs and, ultimately, not supported by their budget. The drawings I prepared included the features and items I believed they wanted, and the multiple bidder process identified a lowest price for the work.

However, this effort rapidly escalated into a very cumbersome, frustrating, and expensive exercise whenever a low bid exceeded the available budget. My use of this traditional design-bid-build process sometimes became the design-bid-redesign-rebid-construction process. Once the preferred bidder revealed the detailed costing, I would revisit all preferences and selections with my client and contractor, suggest alternatives, rearrange and reduce the project scope, and otherwise modify the drawings to accurately reflect all changes before a final re-pricing. This second effort was both time consuming and emotionally exhausting.

Crisply proportioned French country details compatibly integrated with natural stone into the Virginia hillside.

unlike adjusting an individual track on a recording studio soundboard. The technician focuses on a single track of the overall mix, and makes subtle adjustments that affect the final outcome.

The cost of each material selection, customized feature, and fixture can be equated to the hundreds of individual dials and dozens of equalizer slide bars on a soundboard. The seemingly simple adjustment of volume, bass, and treble for a single instrument or voice, when combined with all of the other inputs, becomes quite complicated. The final recording is not released for play (construction) until the overall mix (final drawings) of all tracks (selections) has been artfully adjusted and approved. For your house, these settings represent the quantity, quality, and cost of each specific selection, including customized items. The "final cut" that is released represents the final drawings used for construction.

Custom residential design involves balancing many variables. Knowing the individual cost is an important part of deciding each selection. When an item seems too pricey, lower-cost alternatives are readily considered. This selection-feedback decision process is not

I knew the key to processing better design and making decisions on selections was the procurement of price feedback as a decision tool. Getting such information under the design-bid-build approach proved difficult, if not impossible. It was unreasonable to expect a reputable contractor to invest the 40 or more hours required to pre-bid a project, with only a one in three—or less—chance of winning the final bid.

One immediate option was for me to consider the design-build process and become my own contractor. This was problematic for me, as I found my plate was consistently full with just the concerns and demands of practicing architecture; there was no room for adding the contractor's responsibilities. It had taken me decades of education and experience to reach a comfortable level of professional competence just with architecture. I can only imagine how much longer it might take to also reach a comparable level with contracting. So, I needed to find a more reliable method of sharing anticipated prices, but one that did not require mastering an additional learning curve.

My solution is a hybrid approach combining the economic discipline of competitive bidding with the advantages of ready access to craftsmen and accurate pricing during the detailed design and selection process. My clients select a specific contractor after schematic design, and the contractor provides cost feedback for decisions before I begin preparing the final drawings. By selecting the contractor early, both he and his craftsmen can now safely invest the time required to estimate costs, knowing that they will most likely have the job. The economic checks and balances of competitive bidding remains but moves down a notch from general contractors to a level between material suppliers and multiple subcontractors.

Clear and Open Communication

The best way to keep your process on track and in line with your goals is to maintain frequent, candid, and open communication between all parties involved. The design and construction process, typically, requires many months and thousands of decisions. In addition to presentations, phone calls, and site visits during construction, I strongly recommend that you insist upon access to a digital record of important project documents, communications, drawings, and progress photographs. We currently subscribe to a cloud program for this purpose. We upload PDFs of all drawings, from schematics through final drawings, including any changes or modifications after construction begins. These are made available to you, the contractor, and subcontractors, and are accessible 24/7.

This form of open access to a "project filing cabinet" lessens misinterpretations, misunderstandings, and mistakes. What was agreed to, what was intended, and what was observed become part of a searchable record that lessens the inaccuracies, unreliability, and expensive disagreements that can happen when the parties involved solely rely upon conflicting individual memories.

Kevin's Design Philosophy

IT'S ABOUT YOU, NOT ME

People often ask me, "What is the Kevin Harris style?" Truth be told, there isn't a single Kevin Harris style. Rather, it is more of an approach to how I design. For some architects, perfecting a single or signature style is a great business model that can produce lovely homes. I don't, however, practice architecture through progressively tailored versions of a single style. Instead, I prefer an open design process where the style results from the natural expression of you, your culture, your site, and the region in which you live.

My designs always begin with the functions—that is, the unique working needs of your family—and then gradually progress toward an expression of your style. As a result, the homes I create are as rich in personality as their owners. My passion as an architect is to design homes so well suited to the home owners that their house would be immediately identified by a close friend driving for the first time down the homeowners' street.

Some architects sell drawings only, but we're a full-service firm, so I prefer to stay involved from the first site visit to the final nail. There is so much that can be lost in the process of interpreting a set of plans that I believe the best value and result is for the author of those plans to be involved until the house is fully realized. This is the best way to ensure an accurate translation.

FROM TUSCAN VILLA TO CLASSIC SOUTHERN

If you look through my portfolio, you'll find that over the course of 30 years of design work, no two of my projects quite look the same. This is because the likes and dislikes of my clients are always varied, and I thrive on the challenge of designing homes that reflect and celebrate those distinctions. I have a deep appreciation for a wide range of architectural styles and love the creativity involved in designing a home that resonates, at the deepest level, with you and your family.

Kevin's Top 10 Design "Dos"

1. Do follow the hierarchy of design in your decision making.

2. Do bring your own culture and uniqueness to your project.

3. Do design your house to nestle into a specific site.

4. Do create flow throughout the home without traffic bottlenecks.

5. Do plan for the future.

6. Do design for timelessness. Avoid the temporary vitality of a passing fad.

7. Do design with durable, low-maintenance materials.

8. Do design for energy efficiency.

9. Do use proportions to guide your composition, sizing and locating each element to complement the whole.

10. Do design your house to become your forever home.

A mix of arches come together to orchestrate an elegant entry sequence.

CHAPTER FOUR

It Takes a Team

"Coming together is a beginning. Keeping together is progress. Working together is success."

—HENRY FORD

Teamwork is the common ingredient found in every successful industry, sports, and construction effort. Predicting the future performance of a team begins by analyzing who actually fills the roster. You are the team owner and your architect is the team's general manager, the one who helps outline your program of objectives to guide the design.

The owner, architect, and contractor make up the core team. When interiors and landscaping must be budgeted for a later date, this trio is also the bare minimum you will need. However, when creating a forever home, and when the budget allows, I recommend drafting a full design team, including interior and landscape designers, to participate during design development.

Although each is a specialist in his or her field, there is a good deal of overlap in design scope between design professions. When the interior and landscape designers are given the opportunity to collaborate with the architect early in the process—for example, during design development—it frequently results in cohesive synergistic solutions. Collaborative design is, in many ways, a process of negotiation. After your requirements are defined, the diverse perspectives, expertise, and competing objectives between each designer will be hammered out to influence the final result in positive, robust, and unforeseen ways.

Next on your forever home team roster is the contractor, who acts as the construction team captain. Long before construction begins, he will work with the architect to troubleshoot development of the schematic design and explore more accurate preliminary costing.

A drop zone by the family entrance provides a quiet place to read a book, slip on shoes, or stage items to and from the garage.

Who Chooses the Team?

You do. Period. You can get input from sources and rely on the professional advice, but this effort is about your house and spending your money, so you are the one who chooses which designers and contractors will best serve your interests. Others recommend or suggest, but legally, you choose.

Where to Scout Potential Players?

Sorting through a list of locally available alternatives is a good place to start your search. If not all of the skill and expertise you need is available within your own town, widen the geographic scope. Sources to build your initial roster should include referrals solicited from among friends, family, realtors, and from the occasional Sunday drive past houses under construction. Add Internet and magazine searches to your quest to increase the geographic circle of potential players.

Inviting outsiders into a local mix, however, adds the challenge of coordinating face-to-face meetings. Much collaborative work can be done virtually, but personal interaction between the designers is often necessary to improve rapport and accelerate the trust-building process of defining tasks, managing participant expectations, and creating engagement methods for productive teamwork. Scheduling meetings is managed through an organized schedule that includes clarification of individual designer responsibilities. Your architect should lead this organizational process.

The majority of communication on any project today is handled through phone, mail, and Internet correspondence. Physical meetings are infrequent. This makes it more feasible to consider utilizing remote professionals. Out-of-town participants only need to travel for critical reviews. These occur at design formation, detail resolution, and periodically, to confirm implementation during construction. Advances in information technology make communications manageable, transparent, and efficient frequent use of digital cameras and cell phones. I am able to monitor daily progress between monthly payment approval visits through detailed photographs and telephone discussions. The bulk of the communication runs as efficiently as if the construction were in town.

Here are some of the typical ways people scout to find building professionals today.

Referrals

Friends and family: Your friendship circle is likely to offer a broad set of recommendations for designers and contractors to consider. This group is also a source for construction experience narratives and best practices to use or avoid.

Your architect: Ask the architects you interview to share names of other design professionals and contractors they have worked with and would be happy to recommend. Likewise, ask the contrac-

Separate vanities accommodate competing schedules in a master bath.

for the out-of-town professionals included on your team. I have experienced great success throughout construction while being removed several states from the construction. Responsible monitoring was possible through

tors you meet to share their preferred list of architects.

Realtors: Successful real estate professionals are a reliable source of information on the capabilities and reputations of local designers and contractors. They also are knowledgeable about building restrictions and permitting concerns, and can provide you with a list of homeowners willing to share their personal construction experience and lessons learned.

Internet

Professional association sites: Organizations that regulate the business of each profession provide contact information on their members. Check out the local, state, and national component sites for architects, interior designers, landscape architects, and contractors, and get a feel for who is available. Most organizational sites also feature a member locator list with contact and website information.

Individual company sites: Conduct a web search to identify individuals practicing in your region. Review their information, testimonials, and portfolio, and search the local or state industry honors and awards listed. A fair-sized collection of honors tends to indicate peer recognition of quality work, a perceived innovativeness, and a high level of talent.

Association Websites

AIA: American Institute of Architects–www.aia.org/

NAHB: National Association of Home Builders–www.nahb.org/

ASID: American Society of Interior Designers–www.asid.org/

ASLA: American Society of Landscape Architects–www.asla.org/

MAGAZINES

Magazines featuring custom residential projects fill the shelves at bookstores and supermarkets and can be found on countless coffee tables. Quality work in local and regional publications provides a legitimate third-party endorsement of design talent, so it's something to consider adding to your search list. The professionally shot photographs are also a great medium for you to capture any desirable room atmospheres, or material and color combinations you like. Magazine clippings are a great way to communicate your preferences to your designers and contractor.

SUNDAY DRIVE

Take time to schedule a few peaceful hours to become more in touch with the city, neighborhood, and countryside where you intend to create your forever home. Make note of any ongoing building projects that interest you. Look for lawn signs identifying the contractor and architect involved. Many clients come into my office after seeing one of my signs posted in front of a project they admired. If you like what you see, find out who was responsible and add that person to your list.

Team Selection Criteria or Try-Outs

Collecting the names of candidates for your team is the first step. Reducing your interview list down to a manageable number comes next. How best to filter through all of these names? My recommendation is to obtain enough information about each candidate that will allow you to sort through and compare individual qualifications, design sensibilities, and reputations. Much is readily available on their websites, where you can access information on each company's history, philosophy, past projects, phone numbers, and e-mail.

You will soon have ample criteria to cull down your list to a manageable handful of promising possibilities. Through telephone calls and personal visits, you can then interview the candidates on this list to further assess individual demeanor, personality, current workload, and availability for your project.

Opposite left: The right team of craftsmen can make a project great. Authentic columns were molded in place beside pulled plaster and custom ironwork.

Opposite right: This column, displayed in the family room, was proudly signed by the entire design and construction team.

Cross-check your list with consumer protection agencies, starting with the local branch of the Better Business Bureau, to identify any unsavory characters who have somehow managed to avoid word-of-mouth discovery.

This is your home, and it is all about you. The designers I suggest you select should be ready and willing to incorporate your personality and lifestyle into their creative solutions. No matter the degree of prestige, talent, or ability an individual may possess, each should demonstrate a willingness to work with your chosen team and to share the common goal of producing your forever

A gentle arch becomes a portal into an uncomplicated world where one can relax, bathe, and enjoy serenity, calmness, and order. A place where everything is always as is should be.

home. Above all, you should go with your gut feelings and select individuals you like, as you will be working with them for one or more years.

To help with your selections, here are attributes you should consider.

BASIC QUALIFICATIONS

Education and experience: Get the facts on your team members' education and related work experience. Note where they show particular talent or interest in items that will directly affect your project or indicate a level of reliability or professionalism.

Licensure: Verify that each team member is properly licensed or registered and has an up-to-date permit to work in your project's location. Each state issues licenses to architects as well as to contractors. Some municipalities may also require local licensure for contractors and subcontractors.

DESIGN SENSIBILITIES

Beauty is always in the eye of the beholder, and designs regarded as beautiful by some are considered ugly to others. This inconsistency can be attributed to individual interpretations and beliefs in aesthetics, which determine one's design sensibility. It is imperative that the designers who will create your forever home reflect your design sensibility, and understand how to best provide pleasure, identity, and meaning.

A good way to discern if a candidate's design sensibility is compatible with yours is to review the portfolio section of that candidate's website, illustrating past projects. Ask yourself if you can see your future house included in the mix. Not all architects share my approach of developing a unique style tailored to each individual client. I recommend that you eliminate any designers whose past work does not resonate with your preferences.

REPUTATION

Understanding how others perceive your candidate can give you an idea of what to expect in terms of design quality and levels of service. Reputations provide insight into how someone is esteemed in the eyes of both customers and peers.

Request a list of their past clients and follow up with these references to gain insight about their experience. Was your candidate easy to work with and responsive throughout the project? Also, inquire about how conflicts were resolved. Were they diplomatic or confrontational? Were those clients pleased with the end results?

INTERVIEWS

The information, web searches, and referrals you gather will determine which candidates are qualified. Interviews will determine who is best for your forever home.

After introducing yourself and your goals, be prepared to ask detailed questions that require specific answers.

How your candidates respond will provide insight into their demeanor and personality, and ultimately determine if they are a good fit for you and your team.

It is important to determine your candidates' interest level in your project. Is your project the right size and complexity for their company, or is it too big, too small, or too custom? Determine their current workload, and when they anticipate availability for an additional project. Ask about the size of their staff and the typical number of concurrent projects. Knowing how many projects they work on at any one time, divided by the number of staff, will give you an idea of the attention your project is likely to receive. Also, inquire about fees, how they are determined, what is included, and what is considered extra.

QUALITY

For both architects and contractors, go and see their homes currently under construction. Spend a few hours, unrushed and on your own time schedule, to investi-

A private, spa-like retreat with calming colors and relaxing
textures can bring serenity to demanding lifestyle.

The words light, clean, and bright drove the design solution to this forever home master suite.

gate projects referred to you as illustrative of a candidate's design or construction ability.

If the home is still under construction, take note of the neatness of the contractor's work site, lack of trash, and organization of materials waiting for assembly. A properly supervised construction crew will have an orderly site. This is also usually a good indication that you will find quality workmanship inside. A messy site often indicates inadequate supervision and lack of attention to seemingly minor (but tellingly important) details, and likely reflect an absence of quality assurance measures and fine craftsmanship.

For homes that have been completed before your visits, use the reference contact information and call ahead to view the property with or without the designer or contractor present. While you tour the work, interview the owner to learn about their experience, overall satisfaction with the professionals involved, any problems the project encountered, and results of their resolution.

A good sign is when a former client is inclined to use again, or recommend, the same professional or craftsman. Custom residential design and construction is a reputation-driven industry. Assessing customer satisfaction is the best source for confirming a referral.

TRUST

What does your "gut" say? Would you feel comfortable working with this team member? Do you trust this person's professionalism?

If the answer is yes, great. That gut feeling, coupled with your due diligence homework, is about as optimal a chance you can give yourself for a successful project.

There are no guarantees in life or construction that everything will go smoothly. You will be working with this person for a one- to two-year period. It is important that you like him or her.

If your gut says no, I suggest you reconsider.

Low trust in a business relationship is simply too costly, financially as well as emotionally. The *Harvard Business Review* and Steven Covey have both published articles on the high costs of lost (low) trust within a single business organization.

I have witnessed that these principles apply in a construction setting as well.

When there is baseline trust, and open and transparent communication, projects run more smoothly, and issues that arise are addressed appropriately and put to rest in a timely fashion. Collaboration is improved with better results and less anxiety.

However, when there is a lack of trust, or a breach of trust, among the parties, there are increases in time, costs, and anxiety. Symptoms of a low-trust project include lack of transparency in communication, hidden agendas (often aided and abetted by lack of transparency), increased paperwork and risk management, and increased oversight and redundancy, to name a few. Maintaining this type of atmosphere is financially and emotionally toxic. This situation also lowers the speed of a project. And time is money.

I say this not because trust alone covers all. You are well advised to confirm that trust, as expressed in the Russian adage that President Reagan quoted to Soviet President Gorbachev during arms negotiations, "Doveryai, no proveryai," or in English, "Trust but verify." Within any business transaction there should be safeguards, rules, processes, and procedures to bolster trust. You should know what to expect throughout the process. I am a fan

Bar stools comfortably accommodate guests in this open kitchen and reconnects the cook with the dinner party.

of transparency, in which dealings and communication are accessible, so all parties can verify for themselves. This way trust is built in and built upon.

Creating a High-Performance Team

"The way a team plays as a whole determines its success. You may have the greatest bunch of individual stars in the world, but if they don't play together, the club won't be worth a dime."

—BABE RUTH

After selecting your forever home team, what next? How do you get the team members to begin "playing" together on your house? A productive team is one where the members become unified partners, each sharing the same goals and providing communal support. Managing this effort requires everyone to be on the same page and pulling in the same direction.

When your forever home team first comes together, don't be surprised if the team goes through some growing pains on the way to becoming your high-performance, forever-home dream team. There are four typical stages teams go through: form, storm, norm, and perform. Form begins with the selection process of your key professionals. They learn the specific goals of your project and desired outcome. Storm is the stage at which team members experience "rubs" as they navigate and figure out the optimal way to communicate and get comfortable with boundaries, limitations, and overlap. The fact that a team may go through a period of "storming" should not be a surprise. The more professional and competent the team members are, the less signs of storm you may detect. The norm stage is where the team understands each member's roles, relationships, and standards. Finally, in the perform stage, the team is able to function together for the common goal and to find ways to get work done smoothly without inappropriate conflict. Your contract and contract documents are designed to facilitate getting through this process quickly.

In addition to the contract and contract documents, I find that proactively addressing role definition, team structure, and project communication enhances team cohesion.

Role Definition

There are many grey areas in the design process where material decisions and features that are the responsibility of one professional overlap with those of another. For example, the architect will design the structure and recommend materials for the walls, flooring, cabinetry, and lighting. The interior designer may also make recommendations for the materials and finishes of these same elements. Who is ultimately responsible for the selections? And is it the interior designer or the contractor who is to procure these? If something does not fit or is ordered twice, or incorrectly, who is expected to make the correction? Will you be charged extra for these mistakes?

Clarifying the expected role and responsibility of each team member up front will go a long way toward avoiding these conflicts. Request that your architect review with you appropriate alternative roles for the design team, as on a house, many of these design roles can overlap. Deciding which recommendation should guide that aspect of the house should be hammered out between the designers before being presented to you for a decision. For example: Competing suggestions for materials, fixtures, and finishes must be decided and communicated to the entire team as your final selections. This will help eliminate expensive miscues, misunderstandings, and heartache later during construction.

Team Structure

Your team will design and build your forever home. While everyone should be fully engaged throughout the project, there are ample challenges of complexity and management during each phase to warrant two leaders: one for design, and one for construction. The design leader is the architect, and the construction leader is the contractor.

Design: All of your designers should coordinate their efforts, recommendations, and construction documents with the architect. This includes whatever engineering, interior design, landscape, audio and video, lighting, kitchen, closet, or home automation features you wish to incorporate. Hammering out expected tug-of-war issues between design professionals and their competing sensibilities will forge a complimentary design resolution superior to what each might have contributed on their own. Led by the architect, this collaboration becomes focused on what must be included, or edited out, to accomplish the common objective of designing, building, furnishing, and landscaping your forever home. The final set of construction documents that the contractor will rely upon to obtain price proposals, schedule work, and direct craftsmen should include all of these parts, features, and expected quality levels.

Construction: The construction team leader is the contractor, who is charged with ordering all supplies and materials and scheduling construction work. Because of this, you, your architect, and all members of your design team must resist any and all urges to give directions to the laborers and craftsmen. There should be only one boss on the construction site. Confusion and chaos is the unhappy and expensive alternative.

Project Communications

Insist, from the beginning, that all design team communications must run through the design team leader, your architect. It is among the architect's duties to lead the design effort and coordinate the final results into a comprehensive set of construction documents.

Once these have been priced and construction is underway, all changes, modifications, or adjustments must also be communicated through the architect. The architect will translate these modifications into definitive instructions to the contractor for pricing, approval, and incorporation into the active scope of work.

During construction it is an absolute must that all instructions to the craftsmen, suppliers, and subcontractors can only come through the construction team leader, the contractor.

Following these three communication instructions will save you untold headaches, and greatly minimize the occurrence of communication miscues, additional expenses, unnecessary drama, and time delay.

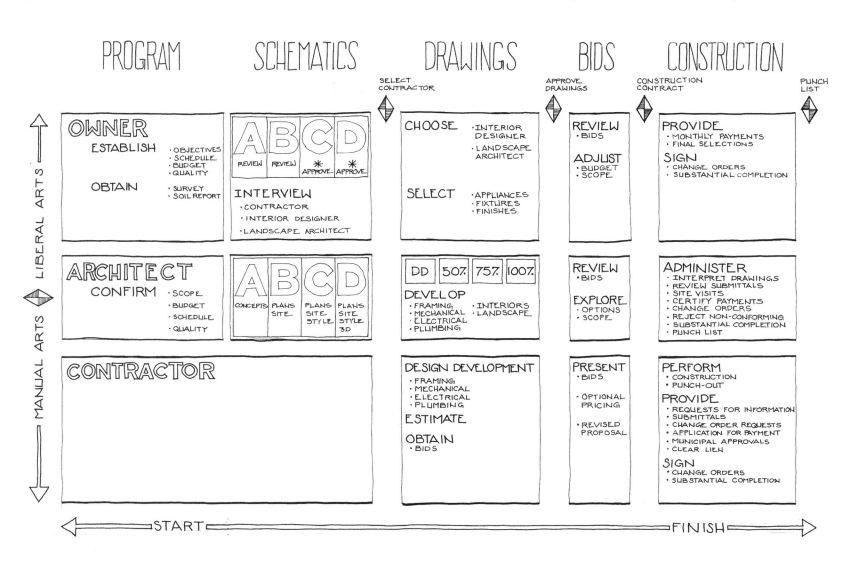

Details cast shadows that make this home as beautiful at night as in the sunlight.

CHAPTER FIVE

The Construction Process

"A work is made in the urging sounds of industry, and, when the dust settles, the pyramid, echoing silence, gives the sun its shadow."

—Louis I. Khan

Construction Step by Step

While each home is unique, simple logic governs the overall sequencing of construction. For example, activity onsite only commences after obtaining a building permit, and wiring follows framing. There is a logical cart-after-the-horse progression that allows work to build upon prior actions.

Installing outside of this order becomes a cart-be-fore-the-horse sequence and can lead to confusion, longer construction time, unnecessary commotion, and increased cost.

Contractors are well aware of this orderly progression. However, they cannot keep to the schedule without having selections decided ahead of related construc-tion. This is especially true with anything custom. The craftsmen must be able to visualize your intended desires, materials, and finishes. This is because it takes time to procure materials, schedule delivery, contract with craftsmen, and choreograph activities at the construction site. Specific placements and connections guide minor adjustments to the overall assembly. Delaying decisions "until later" most often creates forced solutions and awkward results. Take flooring, for example. Choosing a brick floor for the den, hardwood in all bedrooms, and stone tiles for

A seating nook adjacent to an outdoor kitchen provides guests and host a place to enjoy a glass of wine before dinner.

the foyer and kitchen will use materials that come in three different thicknesses, and these will all be on the same walking plane. In order to maintain a level floor, the contractor must adjust his forms to conceal these variations in material thicknesses. Waiting until after the slab is poured to decide on flooring material will reduce your options for materials of the same thickness. Otherwise, the interface between each material will evidence an awkward transition level that also presents a potential trip hazard. These hidden details, options, and results are common when certain decisions come too late to make adjustments.

Even though your entire design team will help you navigate this process, not all homeowners are comfortable making selections before being able to visualize the spaces, and they may want to make changes once the actual construction begins. In these situations, we advise how long each decision might be delayed before the delay adversely limits the possibilities. Your contractor is responsible for scheduling the work and will warn you whenever further delay of a decision becomes disruptive.

Many features require synchronization with earlier work. For example, shower fixtures have mixing valves that are installed inside the walls. The exposed controls selected for design and finish, however, must coordinate with that hidden valve, and the finished surfaces are applied before attaching the controls. Choosing a fixture is rarely an issue before construction begins, as long as its location is definite. However, switching a fixture becomes difficult once the piping and subsequent layers of work are completed between the valve and the controls. Changing the fixture can require demolishing a wall to gain access to the original valve for removal and replacement, followed by reconstruction of the demolished finishes.

It's understandable for you to make minor adjustments during construction. A forever home is going to be your permanent home, and I realize how important it is for you to get things as close to perfect as possible. Just don't be surprised when late decisions and changes increase your construction costs.

The Construction Contract

It is equally important for you to get the house you want at the price you have negotiated as it is for the contractor to have a clear understanding that what he has priced conforms to your expectations. The architect's plans and specifications define the issues of quantity, quality, and arrangement, and your construction contract covers those items of timely delivery, payment, and provisions for procedures and consequences should things go wrong.

Traditional construction contracting involves three parties: owner, contractor, and architect, and two separate contracts, one between the owner and the architect, and one between the owner and the contractor. There is no contract between the architect and the contractor. There is a confusion of contracts available for construction projects, so I recommend using the standard AIA contracts. The AIA has been refining construction contracts for over 150 years in an effort to provide legal terms and language that address the situations most likely to occur, while remaining balanced and fair to all parties involved. They are periodically updated by advocates representing owners, contractors, and architects, and are an industry standard. Each outlines specific duties, responsibilities, and relationships between owner, contractor, and architect.

The major items to consider in any construction contract include:

1. *Scope of work:* which deliverables from each party are included in the contract, which is defined in the drawings and specifications and made part of the contract agreement

2. *Construction time:* when construction will begin, what period of time is allowed, and how liquidated damages are to be determined if the work takes longer to complete that an agreed-upon period

This comfortable arcade connects to the garage and doubles as an ideal entertaining space in inclement weather.

5. *Insurance:* details of insurance that the contractor provides, and what the owner provides because none of the others have them;

6. *Roles of the owner, contractor, and architect:* clear definition of the duties, responsibilities, and limits of authority of each participant in the process

7. *Changes:* how changes to the work will be communicated, processed, and paid

8. *When things go wrong:* how to correct nonconforming work, what to do when unknown conditions are encountered, and how to terminate the contract

9. *Substantial completion, final completion, and final payment:* what is required to certify each of these stages and clarify the resultant shifts in liabilities, warranties, and insurance coverage

3. *Contract sum:* how much the construction will cost, including allowances to obtain or install certain items, and unit prices for items for which the specific quantity is unknown

4. *Payment:* how the contractor is to be paid and how often, provisions for certification of amounts due, and how to determine any withholding amounts

The Architect's Role

Architects wear numerous hats. One of the challenges of being, and of working with, an architect is to under-

A hint of grass, outdoor dining, and an enclosing arcade combine to create this relaxing courtyard.

stand the three distinct roles that the architect is required by law to perform throughout the design and construction process. Each comes with its own set of responsibilities and all standard AIA documents clarify the positions, duties, and authority of each.

➤ *Independent contractor:* The architect furnishes architectural services for which the owner agrees to pay a fee.

➤ *Owner's agent:* The architect has the authority to act, in a limited fiduciary capacity, to represent the owner's interests during construction.

> *Quasijudicial officer:* The architect interprets the design and construction documents and judges the performance of the owner and the contractor under the terms of the contract, without bias to or for either party.

During construction, the architect is considered a "friend of the contract." He or she interprets a balanced compliance with the contractual provisions that is fair to all sides. As a fiduciary agent, he or she looks out for the client's best interests and works with the contractor to guide the end result, while also protecting the client against work that is unacceptable or does not follow the plans.

To deliver these services the architect will

1. keep the client informed of the progress;

2. administer the construction contract;

3. visit the site at appropriate intervals during construction;

4. review and certify payments due to the contractor;

5. reject unacceptable and nonconforming work;

6. review shop drawings, product data, samples, and similar submittals from the contractor for conformance with the design;

7. interpret and decide matters of performance required by the contract;

8. show no partiality with interpretations or decisions.

Your Emotions: What to Expect

You're up. You're down. You're irked one day, ecstatic the next! Welcome to the emotional roller coaster of a construction project.

Over the years, I have found that every client, no matter how even-tempered, experiences a tumbling jumble of emotions while the home is being built. Perhaps that's

Colonnades, insect screens, and an exterior kitchen support a year-round entertaining lifestyle common along the semi-tropical Gulf Coast.

Broad verandas shade interiors while providing for outdoor entertaining. Wide steps announce "welcome to our home" and stage countless group photos.

not surprising, given the emotional investment in a home. But what is surprising is that these highs and lows prove so predictable you can track them on a chart.

To help my clients grasp this, I always give them a copy of the "Funk Chart" the first time we meet. It's a whimsical graph that helps them manage their expectations during the wild ride ahead.

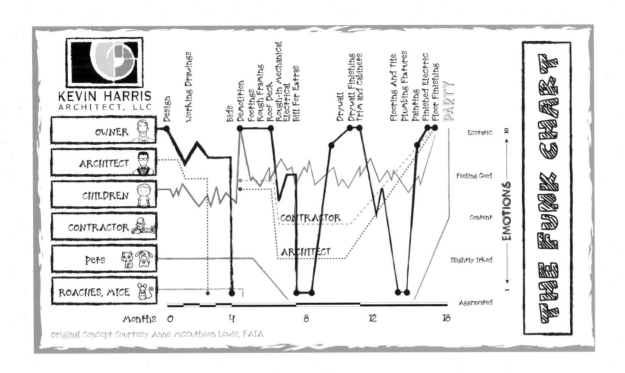

The Funk Chart — an emotional road map showing OWNER, ARCHITECT, CHILDREN, CONTRACTOR, Pets, and ROACHES, MICE over Months 0 to 18, with phases including Design, Working Drawings, Bids, Demolition, Footings, Rough Framing, Roof Deck, Rough-In Mechanical, Electrical, Bill For Extras, Drywall, Drywall Finishing, Trim and Cabinets, Flooring And Tile, Plumbing Fixtures, Painting, Finished Electric, Floor Finishing, PARTY. Emotions scale from Aggravated to Ecstatic.

KEVIN HARRIS
ARCHITECT, LLC

Original Concept Courtesy Anne McCutcheon Lewis, FAIA

I first came across the Funk Chart after a colleague, Anne McCutcheon Lewis, FAIA, gave a talk at the Smithsonian in Washington, DC. The concept rang so true that I asked for permission to use the chart in my own practice. I've tweaked and modified it over the years, but it's based on Anne's original concept.

Emotional Road Map

I love the Funk Chart because it helps you visualize the entire process of building or renovating a home, starting with the architectural drawings and moving on through pricing, demolition, and framing, until you finally reach the last turn of the doorknob and the celebration party. While the Funk Chart was designed to illustrate emotions during a renovation, I have found it to be an equally accurate prediction during new construction.

The right-hand side of the chart details the full range of emotions you'll experience as you move through the building or remodeling process, from a low of seriously aggravated to a high of off-the-chart ecstatic.

Best of all, it shows which emotions you can expect to feel when, with graph lines depicting the roller coaster ride for everyone involved, including you, me, the kids, and the family dog.

Bad news: You'll feel irked and aggravated at times. Good news: Those emotions are short lived and completely normal at some phases in the process.

Predictable Dips and Peaks

Normally, clients always feel good at the design phase but become agitated when they receive the construction prices, even if the cost matches their budget. Why? Because a home is usually a family's biggest investment and making this major decision can be stressful.

On the flip side, I've found that clients always feel ecstatic when the roof and windows seal the house and the drywall installation begins. They feel that "it's starting to look like a home!" But black clouds drift down during the flooring, tiling, and cabinet installation phases when they ask, "Why is this taking so long?"

While the ups are great, the downs can take an emotional toll. Some clients become so anxious they want to

fire everyone, stop the project, and flee to a Pacific island. If that happens to you, get out the Funk Chart, take a deep breath, and remind yourself, "Hmm, I'm right on target; Kevin told me this would happen. It's all part of the process."

Trust me, if you've selected an architect and a contractor with good track records, it will all be okay. I promise my clients that I'll remind them as we go through the process, and before they know it, they'll be back to ecstatic, wildly in love with their new home and ready to throw a celebration party.

As for the kids, the architect, and the family dog, at the end, they're feeling ecstatic too. The only ones left unhappy are the rodents and pests because they were driven off during site clearing.

An easily-accessible outdoor kitchen ensures maximum convenience and use.

Client Decision Making during Construction

During a construction project there are various crossroads where the owner is required to weigh in, select, or authorize materials and work. Examples could include the deferred selection of plumbing fixtures, finish materials, or the resolution of unforeseen options (or surprises) in the construction process, just to name a few.

Keeping the project on schedule requires the owner to make timely decisions. Any decision delays can unintentionally extend the contractor's time for completion and thus the cost for construction. The time pressure of making mid-construction decisions, coupled with a typical homeowner's unfamiliarity with options presented, can lead to anxiety and delays. Your architect and design team can help you navigate the selection process and avoid extended delays by helping you analyze the pros and cons, and make timely decisions on preferred options.

Payments during Construction

The AIA contract outlines a standard method for submittal, approval, and payments to the contractor during construction.

CONTRACTOR'S APPLICATION FOR PAYMENT

Most contractors submit a monthly AIA application for payment to the architect. This document reconciles the schedule of values assigned to each scope-of-work element with the work in place, the work completed since the most recent payment, and the work remaining. Each application is then reviewed by the architect and compared to onsite observation of actual work performed. The architect can either accept the application or reject

Masterfully crafted brick parapets, arches, and fireplaces provide visual interest and elegantly punctuate interior and exterior functions.

it, sharing his reasons with the contractor and requesting modification and resubmittal.

CERTIFICATE FOR PAYMENT

If the architect accepts the request for payment, he or she will create and sign a certificate that begins the process of payment to the contractor. The certificate of payment represents that the work has progressed to a point in accordance with the contract documents to the best of the architect's knowledge, information, and belief. The contract will specify a set number of days after approval, within which the owner must pay that sum to the contractor.

Because of the natural stone's variations and the ever-changing patterns of sunlight, the façade looks different every time you look at it.

As there is no contract between the architect and the contractor, payment does not flow through the architect. Payments go directly from the owner to the contractor.

RETAINAGE

I normally recommend disclosing, in the owner-contractor contract, the provision to withhold a predetermined percentage of the work completed as a retainer. This is to protect the owner against any unfinished work at the end of the project. Accumulated retainage is partially released following substantial completion, and the remainders are incrementally released as punch-list items (unfinished work) are completed.

The architect can also recommend withholding payment amounts when portions of the work are defective, or if it is discovered that subcontractors or suppliers have not been paid by the contractor for their completed work on your project.

CLARIFICATIONS DURING CONSTRUCTION

The very term *custom residential design* suggests choices or detailing unique to your home. Each custom home is an individual prototype and, as such, has never been built before. Although designed to include rational building practices and available materials, some features may be unfamiliar or unclear to the craftsmen. Clear communication between the contractor and architect about expectations is important. The contractor must let the architect know whenever more information or clarification is needed to guide the work before proceeding, as it is the contractor who is solely responsible for the means, methods, and sequencing of the construction.

Clarification occurs throughout the construction process in the following ways:

1. *Request for information:* This is a standard method in construction whereby the contractor describes, for the architect to clarify, specific

questions with the drawings, the specifications, or other related construction expectations.

2. *Job site visits:* The architect will visit the construction site periodically throughout construction to become generally familiar with the progress and quality of the work.

3. *Field reports:* These are periodic written reports informing the owner about the progress of construction, the quality of the completed work, and any observed deviations, defects, or deficiencies.

Adjustments during Construction: Change Orders

During your custom home's construction, you will gain a heightened awareness of the many quality levels available. As spaces begin to take physical form, you can also visualize them in a different way. You may discover additional options that promise to better satisfy one or more of your desires. Before making any changes, however, consult with your architect to determine how the change or enhancement might ripple through the seemingly unrelated complexities. Some changes are welcome improvements and can be seamlessly incorporated into the construction. Others can become more involved and costly, and some should be avoided altogether. Exercise caution when considering changes as they may initiate a domino effect, causing an unintended chain reaction of additional work.

I don't encourage changes after construction begins. However, I understand it is a common occurrence. Keeping everyone informed of any changes presents its own challenge and underscores the importance of clear communications during construction. I recommend written modifications and additional drawings, as required, to articulate what is expected in the change order. That is the proper method for modifying a construction contract scope of work, cost, or duration. This involves submitting descriptions and designs for the owner's approval, clarifying the work, how much it will cost, and how long to extend the construction time. A change order modifies the contract and requires all three signatures from the owner, the contractor, and the architect.

A change order is the clearest way to give the contractor, and his subcontractors, ample notification and directions for incorporating the change as you intended. I formalize all such changes using AIA Document G-701.

Communication during Construction

"No battle plan survives
contact with the enemy."

–HELMUTH VON MOLTKE (1800-1891),
PRUSSIAN ARMY CHIEF OF STAFF
RESTATED BY GENERAL COLIN POWELL,
FOLLOWING THE GULF WAR

The best set of drawings and specifications are much like a battle plan, and communication throughout construction is vital to the success of the design intent. Construction is an often messy and fragmented operation and involves a complexity of tempo-

rary interrelationships working together to achieve a common goal. Keeping everyone on the same page is paramount to avoid glitches. Most construction problems are symptoms caused by a failure in clear communications.

To assure accurate and timely communications during construction, I recommend using the following media:

1. *Field reports:* These should be written by the architect following each site visit, and include notes describing briefly what was observed, any issues or questions, and they should include relevant photographs of the in-progress work. Copies of this report are provided to both owner and contractor.

2. *Telephone and e-mail:* In communications between two parties, it is always important to share project status or discuss construction issues that need to be researched or addressed. However, coordination among multiple parties

can be unwieldy and problematic. Telephone records do not accurately capture what was said or intended, and additional parties must be tracked in order for any messages to be rebroadcast. The opportunities for human error and miscommunication are plentiful. E-mail keeps a record, but messages are received alongside a confusion of competing communications unrelated to your project. Until someone invents an automatic method to efficiently and elegantly filter and organize project e-mails, I do not recommend relying upon e-mail as a primary project management communication method.

3. *Monthly site meetings:* These must be attended by the contractor, owner, and architect, who walk the construction site and review—at a minimum—the work in place, work in progress, issues since the last meeting, decisions pending, and work scheduled. Your architect should prepare an agenda for these meetings and take notes on the discussions, decisions, and assignments for follow-up activities.

4. *Electronic files:* Digital communication continues to improve our ability to collaborate remotely, share information, and reduce errors. Unlike our predecessors in this business, we are not limited to issuing paper copies, and paper modifications to be inserted into those copies, to the many craftsmen and suppliers. In a paper-based system, keeping track of who received which communication, and when, is a major record-keeping challenge. Conflicts between craftsmen and suppliers were birthed in hearsay and resulted in confusion, misunderstandings, or rogue substitutions. Cloud computing eases project communications and reliable file accessibility for all team members. Cloud-based project management sites also reduce redundant efforts and improve individual accountability as members are aware of each other's responsibilities. Current drawings, field reports, and important information can be stored in a virtual filing cabinet that is cloud based, allowing everyone on the project to have ready access to the most up-to-date files. Contractors

confirm that cloud-accessible files reduce subcontractor and supplier confusion, lessening the occurrence of costly construction mistakes. Louis Brandeis likened the transparency of the communication system to "Sunshine... because sunshine is the best disinfectant."

The Construction Triangle: What Owners Can Learn from *If You Give a Mouse a Cookie*

In the triangle of owner-contractor-architect, verbal commitments or explanations are expedient but often misunderstood or forgotten, and are unreliable as a record when it comes to responsibility, accountability, or liability.

As the owner, you are the one writing the checks, and therefore the person ultimately in charge. Because of your power position, anything you request can and will be acted upon by the craftsmen. The hidden

The finishing details of chamfered columns and a soft glow from gas lanterns provide a look of polish and warmth.

> "Be careful not to unwittingly commit yourself, or your project, to unseen implications by saying something as simple as "While you're here..."

questions are (1) at what cost? and, (2) at what level of craftsmanship? Early in my career I encountered situations in which I rejected a material substitution or payment for additional work, only to learn that it had been verbally requested or approved by the owner. Things became particularly problematic when the owner was unhappy with the results. These situations make it difficult, if not impossible, for me to properly administer work directed by the owner outside the construction contract and, more often than not, it resulted in both owner and subcontractor dissatisfaction.

Maintaining a clear communication protocol between owner, contractor, and architect is specified in the AIA documents. These require the owner and the contractor to "endeavor to communicate with each other through the architect." Most construction site directions are given verbally: briefing craftsmen, coordinating vendors, or ordering supplies. Owners must beware that, from the workers' point of view, their boss, the contractor, also has a boss—you, the owner. And should you choose to answer a worker's question, or suggest an enhancement or two on your project, be prepared to accept (and pay for) whatever may result. In the mind of that worker, you have given an instruction and modified the contracted scope of work.

I draw a lesson from the children's book *If You Give a Mouse a Cookie*, written by Laura Numeroff. In this circular tale the mouse makes an initial request to the child for a cookie, which leads to a string of related add-ons because "If you give a mouse a cookie, after all, he's bound to ask for a glass of milk," and then a straw, a mirror, scissors, a broom, and so on, which the child is obligated to take care of. The lesson here is to be careful not to unwittingly commit yourself, or your project, to unseen implications by saying something as simple as "While you're here . . ."

As the AIA contracts suggest, aim to communicate about the project through the architect. This will reduce misunderstandings, create a written record, and help to avoid hidden costs or surprises.

Construction Stages

PRECONSTRUCTION

Zoning, local building codes, restrictive covenants, and other official policies restrict the what, where, and how you can build. Preconstruction approvals can be sought simultaneously or in no particular or-

der. The two most common are the building permit and home owners' association approvals.

Building permit: Municipalities are empowered to adapt and enforce building codes they deem relevant to the protection of health and safety of their citizens. Your local permit office, typically, requires a plan review and approval prior to issuing you a building permit. This confirms that what has been designed is in compliance with locally enforced building codes.

Home owners' association: Subdivisions with restrictive covenants, typically, have architectural committees in place and most require a plan review and association approval before you can start construction. Any of their restrictions are in addition and unrelated to the municipal plan review mentioned above. Check your closing documents for these requirements, or get a copy from your realtor. Neighborhood restrictions are often more restrictive than zoning or building codes and can

An outdoor fireplace and French Quarter-inspired lamps imbue a Louisiana joie de vivre to a forever home in Virginia.

limit or require the use of specific materials and architectural styles.

CONSTRUCTION

The following is a list of major construction milestones that occur sequentially:

1. *Site work:* Clearance of the site and preparing it for construction, plumbing, electricity, water, and gas connections

2. *Foundation:* Installation of wall footings, grade beams, pilings, and/or basement

3. *Framing:* Construction of the walls, floors, and roof structure

4. *Closing, or "drying-in":* Installation of windows, exterior doors, roofing, and other work to seal the exterior from the elements so that work on the interior can begin

5. *Rough-in:* Preliminary installation of plumbing piping, electrical wiring, gas piping, and placement of mechanical equipment

6. *Finishes:* Installation of wallboard, millwork, cabinetry, tile, painting, and other interior decorative work

7. *Top-out:* Final installation of plumbing and electrical fixtures, appliances, and mechanical equipment

8. *Floor finishing:* Application or installation of wood flooring, floor finishes, carpeting, and final clean-up

9. *Final inspections:* Municipal inspectors visit the construction site during key stages of construction to confirm that all work is done in accordance with minimally acceptable standards as specified in the building codes. The final inspection approvals signify an acceptable level of completion.

SUBSTANTIAL COMPLETION

Substantial completion is the project stage at which construction is sufficiently complete for you to safely and legally live in your home. After your home has passed its final building inspection, and you've been granted a certificate of occupancy (if applicable), your architect inspects the home's level of completion and then issues a certificate of substantial completion. This document must be approved and signed by you, the contractor, and the architect. Owners often confuse this stage with final completion and are disappointed that more work is yet to be done, but substantial completion is not final completion. Any remaining construction is completed during the closeout.

Before issuing a certificate of substantial completion, I recommend having the following documents in hand and on file:

1. *Final inspection approvals:* These come from your local municipal building inspectors, including foundation, framing, plumbing, mechanical, electrical, and overall building.

2. *Certificate of occupancy:* These are issued by the local building permit office, certifying

that the building is constructed in accordance with locally enforced building codes.

3. *Punch list:* This is a final tally of construction items to be completed. After the contractor presents to the architect the governmental approvals and a certificate of occupancy, the architect conducts a thorough inspection of the work and prepares a punch list. A punch list typically includes items such as painting touch-ups, misaligned cabinet hinges, or missing light fixtures. These flaws are usually minor and quickly corrected, and rarely prevent owners from beginning to enjoy their new home. Final release of any withheld amounts to the contractor is dependent upon successful completion of the punch list items.

CLOSEOUT

It is important for you to realize that construction is not over once you begin to live in your new home.

Construction closeout takes place when items on the punch list are successfully finished.

The following items are addressed during construction closeout:

1. *Liquidated damages:* When construction takes longer than planned in the construction contract, you are likely to incur additional expenses. One example is finding yourself caught between a home you no longer own and one not yet ready for occupancy, which often involves procuring temporary housing, storing your furniture and household goods, and paying additional interest on your construction loan. Liquidated damages are estimated to offset the monetary injury should construction exceed the contract time. This amount is difficult to estimate, but it should be determined before the contract is signed. Predetermining this amount limits exposure to the liability and protects both you and your contractor. Provisions for liquidated damages must be specified in the construction contract in order to be allowed.

Recycled beams lend texture to clean lines and smooth finishes. Neutral colors expand and relax the space. A comfy sofa provides a convenient place to get dressed, tie shoes, or snuggle a child with a book.

2. *Punch list:* The time frame within which the contractor is allowed to complete punch list items is important. I recommend setting a definite date for completion of the punch list items in the construction contract. One additional month is usually sufficient for the contractor to tidy up all loose ends, advertise

with the clerk of court for a clear lien certificate, as well as assemble all other paperwork and invoices required for review, reconciliation, and approval of the final application for payment.

3. *Final inspection:* After the prescribed time period has expired, I recommend that you

and your architect jointly conduct one last inspection to "punch out" all completed items.

4. *Clear Lien:* A lien is a notice attached to your property's title that claims you owe a creditor. A clear lien is the absence of any claims. Whenever a contractor does not settle all charges for the construction, suppliers, and craftsmen, know that placing a lien on your property is an inexpensive method to secure future collection of what they are owed. Before you can sell or refinance your property, you must have a clear title because most lending institutions will only finance clear titles. A lien on a property makes for an unclear title. Liens in Louisiana are filed with the local clerk of court. To protect owners from the unscrupulous practice of contractors pocketing rather than dispersing received payments, each clerk of court also issues reminders to all unpaid suppliers and craftsmen to file a lien within a specific time frame. Otherwise, they will lose the right to lien your property. They do not, however, lose their rights to pursue payment directly from the contractor. If no liens have been filed before expiration of the filing period, the clerk will issue a clear lien certificate. I recommend requiring the contractor to produce a clear lien certificate for all completed work before final payment. This protects you from paying twice for the same work.

5. *Final payment:* All unpaid contract sums, less any deductions for liquidated damages or unfinished punch list items, are settled at this point. Schedule a one-year warranty inspection on the architect and contractor calendars.

6. *Closure:* This is the event that marks the new beginning, the time when you can fully occupy and enjoy your new home, living without the presence of carpenters, painters, electricians, and other craftsmen underfoot—just you and your family.

Getting to closure requires setting a completion deadline, regardless of whether all items are complete. Anything unfinished is then assigned an estimated cost to complete and deducted from the final payment by your architect.

> "With careful selection of the right contractor beforehand, whenever a few items linger unfinished, most owners choose to have the original contractor finish the work."

There are three possible owner dialogues to address unresolved punch list items after closure and final payment:

1. "Mr. Contractor, I love my house, but I am tired of construction. Give me some time to recover from the commotion, and I will call you when I am ready so that you can have your men come and finish these items. I will pay the sum withheld upon completion of each item";

2. "Mr. Contractor, I love my house, but I am tired of construction. I am also tired of the same old faces that have been unable to complete these remaining items. Therefore, I am going to have someone else complete the work and use the withheld sums to pay them. I will let you know if it costs more, and I expect reimbursement from you. I will also send you a refund if it costs less to complete than was withheld"; or

3. "Mr. Contractor, I love my house, but I am tired of construction. I will simply live with the conditions and keep the money."

I cannot say for certain how these three options motivate the individuals performing the work. I do know that they serve as a safeguard from your being held hostage by someone else's inability to schedule and complete the construction.

All three options are fair to the owner, the contractor, and the architect. Which one you choose is up to you. It has been my experience that, with careful selection of the right contractor beforehand, whenever a few items linger unfinished, most owners choose to have the original contractor finish the work.

Most home construction contracts provide for a one-year warranty for all work. Any repairs necessitated by poor workmanship should be at no additional cost to the owner. I recommend scheduling a one-year inspection on everyone's calendar before the final payment is transferred. In addition, the home owner should be made familiar with all expected operational and maintenance items at that time.

CELEBRATION

It is easy, once you move into your forever home, to be consumed by the long-planned transition and forget to take the time to celebrate, to mark the occasion, and savor the accomplishment. As with other milestones in life, I suggest you take the time to set aside a special date to celebrate, acknowledge, share, and savor the accomplishment.

Perhaps you can have a house blessing, ceremonial lighting of a gas lantern, a dinner party, or a special dessert. Whatever you choose to mark the milestone, do it!

Today, whenever my office completes a project, we mark the end by formally presenting the home owners with a guest book. We inscribe it with my favorite Ralph Waldo Emerson quotation: "The ornament of a house is the friends who frequent it." We encourage homeowners to have visitors sign it. We also suggest they enter in the book descriptions and dates of social events and ask those attending them to sign it. My family is on its third such book, and they have become treasured family heirlooms. Each is a timeless collection of memories, jokes, doodles, and sweet reminders of loved ones, some of whom have passed on.

A Forever Home
Is Never Done

Homes are living, breathing, evolving entities. They are meant to service and support our lives and, as such, are always changing. To accomplish this feat requires planning for adaptability.

As family needs change, a home should change with them. A playroom next to the kitchen might evolve into a music room and can still later morph into a dining room, home office, or library. Give yourself and your home permission to make your spaces support your life.

French doors, outdoor seating, and a spacious rear veranda brings the indoor living experience closer to nature and provides magnificent sunset views.

Stucco, terra cotta tiles, and an exterior arcade transformed an international style home into a Tuscan lakeside villa. Drawing page 141.

Renovation: An Alternative Route to a New Old Home

> *"Renovation is the method by which an older housing stock competes with the new."*

—KERMIT BAKER, HARVARD JOINT CENTER FOR HOUSING STUDIES

One popular alternative to building new is to customize an existing house, in whole or in part, by updating, adding on, or performing surgery. Several terms are used to describe these activities including *remodel, addition, renovation,* and *facelift.* For the purpose of this chapter, I use the term *renovation* to include all modifications or additions to an existing home.

How Renovation Differs from New Construction

In many ways, designing a successful renovation is more complicated than designing from scratch. Unfortunately, people who do not realize how complex the renovation process is often rush into a project unguided. Surrounded by a maze of design options, structural questions, building codes, zoning laws, contractor questions, and so on, most don't understand the value proposition of architectural services until they have stumbled through the process. Blindly renovating without an architect amid these complexities often illuminates the benefits of architectural guidance in planning and managing the construction contract.

Your budget emerges as the primary restriction to your imagination when new construction is involved. Unlike the more predictable canvass of new construction, however, renovations present additional challenges of

A clipped gable, projecting bay, shed dormers, swooping roof, and chimney pots are just a few of the English Tutor elements that blend an addition into the original cottage. Drawing on opposite page.

working within an existing style, unconventional construction, finishes, materials, outdated floor plans, and mature landscaping. The existing conditions must be recorded to study suitable design alternatives and connections. Renovation is similar to performing surgery on a living organism. A complete set of X-rays or an MRI must be procured before planning any surgery. It is critical to know what lies below the skin and hidden from view. It is also necessary to identify features that are to remain undisturbed. All of a home's materials, systems, details, and styles provide the foundation for exploring the feasibility of expansion, incorporation of new materials, and/or floor plan adjustments.

The Renovation Market

The renovation market continues to grow exponentially. Bookstores are filled with magazines on the subject. The Internet overflows with blogs and programs to help organize and share images of spaces and home features. This is because there are so many houses that

EXISTING SOUTH ELEVATION

SOUTH ELEVATION

are due for a facelift. As of 2012, over half the houses in the United States were constructed at least 40 years earlier. Each year, features and finishes become a little older, wear out, or are otherwise outdated. They include kitchens, appliances, bathrooms, and fixtures that were designed for a different way of life. Our standard of living keeps improving, and in order for these homes to accommodate today's lifestyles and higher consumer expectations for comfort, renovations and additions are necessary. Even newer homes are being renovated, especially when designed for a commodity market but lacking the features, finishes, personality, and aesthetics demanded by today's buyers. Renovations and additions can convert old and new houses from boring, characterless quarters into forever homes.

Why Choose Renovation?

The reasons people renovate are as varied as the homeowners themselves. In addition to benefiting you, the investment benefits the neighborhood, the country and, though it sounds like a cliché, the world.

Help stabilize and preserve a neighborhood, its fabric, its value, its livability. A neighborhood where homes continue to be maintained is a sign of good health, just as decaying homes indicate a declining neighborhood.

Preserving this investment in our housing stock is cost-effective and benefits the entire country. The current value of US homes is a staggering $25 trillion. Housing is at the core of strong, vibrant families and communities, and renovating can be less capital intensive than new construction.

Additionally, renovation can be better for the global environment. In the United States, construction debris accounts for approximately one-quarter of all material sent to solid waste facilities. Renovation, as opposed to complete demolition, decreases the load on landfill space, reduces the environmental impact of manufacturing or producing new materials, and can reduce the overall construction expense by avoiding additional material purchases, in addition to disposal costs.

Sounds good, right? But let's put it in everyday terms. Donovan D. Rypkema, principal of Place Economics, provides perspective on the environmental impact of property renovation. He asks us to consider a small, typical, American, shotgun-style home—it could be in New Orleans, Louisiana, for example—located on a lot

Top: A new portico and side expansion add an applied order and symmetry to the existing home.

Bottom: Sloped roofs and shaded colonnades inject the cultural expression of Italian architecture into a recycled international style frame. Photo page 136.

① EXISTING EAST ELEVATION
SCALE 3/16" = 1'-0"

② PROPOSED EAST ELEVATION
SCALE 3/16" = 1'-0"

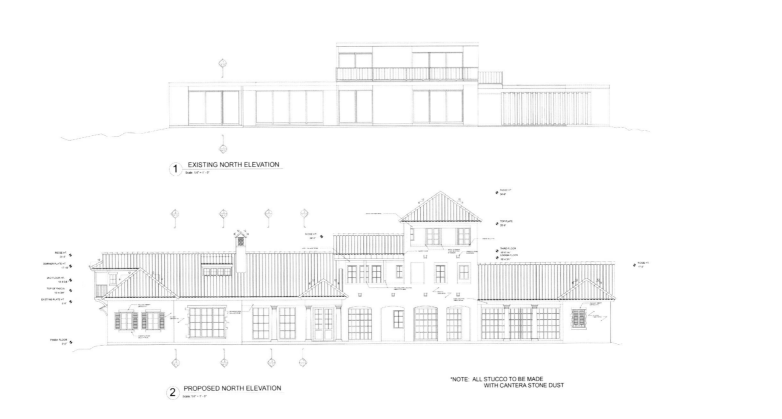

① EXISTING NORTH ELEVATION
Scale 1/4" = 1'-0"

② PROPOSED NORTH ELEVATION
Scale 1/4" = 1'-0"

*NOTE: ALL STUCCO TO BE MADE
WITH CANTERA STONE DUST

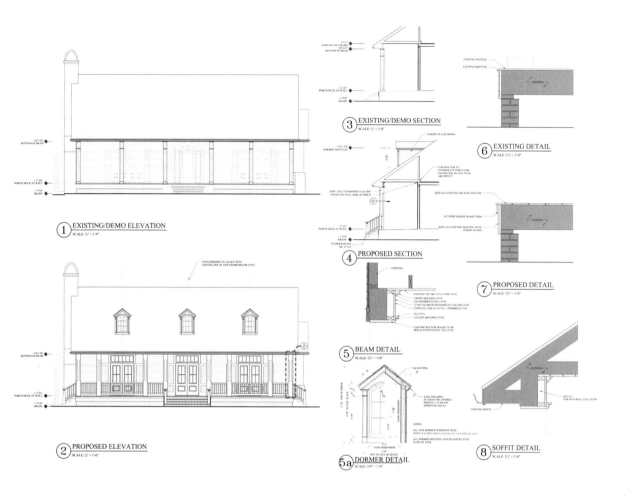

EXISTING/DEMO ELEVATION ①
SCALE: ¼" = 1'-0"

PROPOSED ELEVATION ②
SCALE: ¼" = 1'-0"

EXISTING/DEMO SECTION ③
SCALE: ¼" = 1'-0"

PROPOSED SECTION ④
SCALE: ¼" = 1'-0"

BEAM DETAIL ⑤
SCALE: 1½" = 1'-0"

DORMER DETAIL ⑤a
SCALE: 3/4" = 1'-0"

EXISTING DETAIL ⑥
SCALE: 1½" = 1'-0"

PROPOSED DETAIL ⑦
SCALE: 1½" = 1'-0"

SOFFIT DETAIL ⑧
SCALE: 1½" = 1'-0"

Second floor dormers illuminate and new columns introduce a balanced rhythm to an existing façade. Photo page 16.

Another of Rypkema's studies concludes that when a house is demolished, over 350 tons of raw and waste materials are sent to the landfill, compared to only 50 tons of waste from rehabilitating the original house. In addition to saving 300 tons of landfill waste, the preservation of a single house also greatly lessens the consumption of materials and resources and is a credible way to measure the benefits to the nation of such an exercise.

only 25 feet wide by 120 feet deep. Rypkema draws our attention to the staggering fact that the environmental damage from tearing down just one such building overshadows all the benefits of recycling over 1,344,000 aluminum cans. In fact, his calculations indicate that it takes 35-50 years for an energy-efficient new building to save the amount of energy lost in demolishing an existing building.

What about replacing—as opposed to repairing—single-pane, old-growth, wood-framed windows with insulated-glass, new, aluminum windows? Rypkema puts that in perspective as well. The majority of heat loss in Southern homes is not through the windows but through the attic and walls. Adding three and a half inches of fiberglass insulation in the attic has three times the R factor (a measure of thermal resistance) that replacing a single-paned widow with the most energy-efficient version would have. For example, in our region, the energy savings payback period of replacing a single-paned, wood window with a new, insulated-glass, aluminum window can be as long as 400 years. Rypkema correctly challenges the logic of replacement rather than repair.

Renovation makes your home more livable, but at what cost? Many projects, such as updating the look and function of a kitchen or a bathroom, can offset construction costs by an increase in the home's overall value. Additions add measurable area to a floor plan. Combining thoughtful renovations and additions leverages the improvements' value by multiplying the increase by the entire dollar-per-square-foot equation.

I find that saving as much of what already exists as possible, results in the maximum economy. I also caution against the tendency for the wholesale shredding down to the studs, only to replace with "new." The increase in construction cost would likely exceed what any appreciation in value could possibly counterbalance, resulting in a net loss for the exercise. However, there is one good argument in favor of a whole-house solution; whenever enjoyment of the improvements alone justifies the added expense.

What an Architect Brings to a Renovation

Renovations appear, on their surface, to be simpler than new construction. So much of what you want already exists and any features that are lacking, undesirable, wrong for your tastes, or hamper your lifestyle, are easily identified. The challenge is deciding how to integrate the changes into an existing house.

What does an architect bring to a renovation? Achieving dreamed results requires a seasoned professional to recognize, filter, invent, and finesse a conceptual plan that addresses your lifestyle, amid the visual confusion of existing walls and details. Architects' conceptual advice is based upon their artistic and technical education, practical experience, and understanding of the complex interactions that combine in your house. Even when the work does not warrant detailed drawings, it will benefit greatly from the initial conceptual and schematic guidance of an architect. Architects have an ability to visualize and critically describe the options and share the reasoning supporting the recommendations.

Architects are educated in the formalities of historic composition and can suggest how to renovate in concert with an original design, identify how new elements work with a particular style, and solve any renovation needs, without spoiling the spirit or dignity of your structure. Much of an older home's appeal radiates from its artistic arrangement and details. Understanding historic ornament, proportionally sized and deliberately positioned, becomes paramount. An architect's guidance should minimize any errors in sizing or placement.

An architect is a great resource for the craftsmen tackling an historic structure. Older homes were assembled using techniques, materials, and tools unfamiliar to many of today's craftsmen. The tendency to replace items in the name of expediency is especially unfortunate when an awareness and research can direct a skillful repair instead of a replacement.

Renovation Design Schools of Thought

I prefer seamless transitions between original and new. I believe that every home with a precious identity should emerge from its renovation as a larger, nicer structure. I find updated or enlarged homes that maintain their design spirit are more desirable than the typical result of unrelated add-ons. I encourage compatible additions that avoid the cacophony of unfortunate "remuddles," and include the desirability of compatible additions among my "rules" for renovations.

Importance of the Big Picture

No two renovations are identical, and there is no single, clear-cut path to follow. That is why I recommend a design consultation before any significant renovation. This is a stand-alone service in which I make a house call, investigate the proposed renovation, explore potential options, and leave preliminary drawings that record a preliminary solution and can guide the results. After touring the home and asking critical questions, I pull out my sketch paper, gather the owners around a table and, in an interactive process, begin to explore alternatives. An architect is the one professional who has the education, training, experience, and skills to guide you, relatively quickly, through the numerous opportuni-

> "No two renovations are identical, and there is no single, clear-cut path to follow. That is why I recommend a design consultation before any significant renovation."

ties, obstacles, and limitations, and to integrate your needs into a probable result. The concluding sketches are left with the homeowner to pursue further development or implementation. Design consult services are offered for hourly or fixed fees.

When a client moves ahead, using an architect, these preliminary sketches become the basis for more detailed drawings. I find that these owner-architect interactive sessions reduce the calendar time normally consumed during the standard approach of schematic alternatives.

Determining the Optimal Level of Services

While I am very pro-architect, I am in no way against securing other sources for construction drawings following my design consultations. I

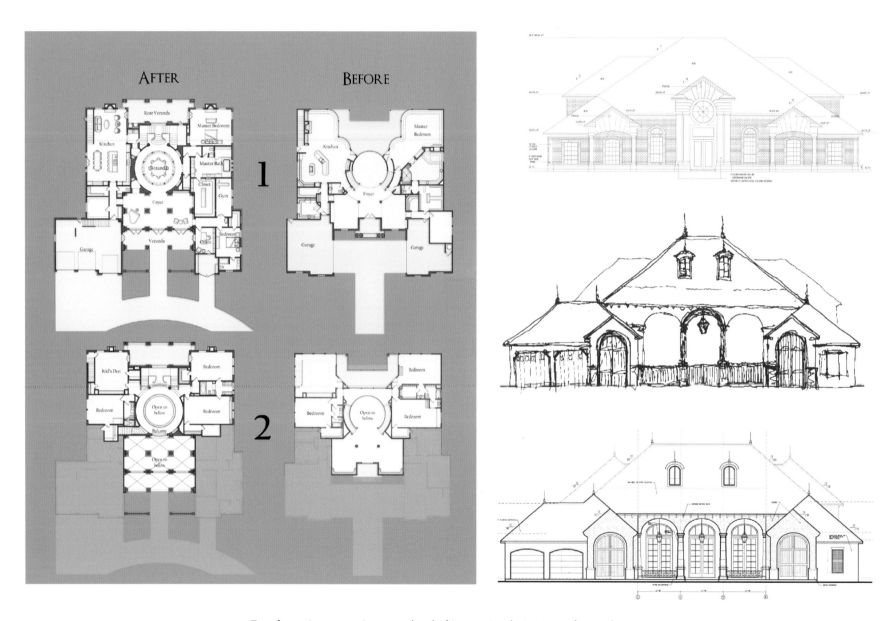

AFTER

BEFORE

1

Rear Veranda

Kitchen

Rotunda

Foyer

Veranda

Garage

Master Bedroom

Master Bath

Closet

Gym

Office

Bedroom

Kitchen

Master Bedroom

Foyer

Garage

Garage

2

Kid's Den

Bedroom

Bedroom

Open to below

Balcony

Open to below

Bedroom

Bedroom

Bedroom

Bedroom

Open to below

Open to below

Bedroom

Bedroom

Transformative renovations morph a drafting service design into a forever home.

recommend purchasing only those services you need. Drawings from a plan service, or other provider, are less expensive than those from an architect. Simple projects with familiar details are appropriate for drafting services or renovation contractors who have the ability to produce their own construction and permit drawings.

Getting the level of architectural services you require is not unlike what you might do to correct a vision problem. If your problem is as simple and common as needing reading glasses, going to the dollar store and self-diagnosing is probably fine. However, when there is more involved, you should elevate the skill level and visit an optometrist for special lenses, or an ophthalmologist for medical services. An architectural renovation follows a similar path. Deciding which level of service is best is about aligning the complexity and customization of your project with the appropriate professional.

One great way to personalize your home is to engage an interior designer. Whenever possible, I encourage working with one early on, as the collaboration of multiple design points of view frequently gives better results. Working together while the design develops is especially important, given the overlap of services offered. Interior designers, not unlike architects, recommend room layouts, door and window positioning, and wall removals in addition to guiding furniture, artwork, finish, fixture, and window covering selections. Too often, interior designers are hired after all major decisions have been finalized, which greatly limits their effectiveness. No amount of appointments or rearranged openings can overcome fundamental errors in the house that conflict with your living patterns. In order to increase the chances of success, I recommend assembling a complete design team: architect, interior designer, and landscape architect. The most successful projects are those benefiting from design collaboration between professionals.

The Go/No-Go Decision

Cost is an important consideration in the decision to leave as is, make minor upgrades, strip to the studs,

> "Deciding which level of service is best is about aligning the complexity and customization of your project with the appropriate professional."

demolish and rebuild, or freshen for resale. Weigh the potential for improvement with other possibilities. Items entering into your cost equation include

- *Cost of renovations:* Proposed renovation costs are the starting point for economic decisions, but are not the sole factor. There are additional expenses that include upgrading interior finishes, furniture, and landscaping.

- *Temporary housing:* During certain phases, construction creates undesirable environments that are difficult or impossible to live in and justify alternative housing. Assess probable costs in your area for leases of one year, six months, or a single month.

- *Time for construction:* Renovations can often be completed in less time than new construction. How important is prolonging or shortening this period of disruption?

- *Sale of existing house:* Is selling your home a realistic option? Do you have the ready cash or equity for another mortgage down payment before a buyer commits?

- *Realtor commission:* Remember to deduct realtor fees from your sale price calculations.

- *Cost of new house:* Benchmark what a new house will cost, and include anticipated realtor's fees to sell your existing home in this cost for a fair comparison.

➤ *Closing costs:* These are in addition to the sales price and, typically, include a property survey, appraisal, title search, closing attorney fee, and loan initiation fee.

➤ *Moving costs:* Unless you are selling your house furnished, add the cost to pack, store, and relocate the contents.

➤ *Cost of tear down:* Demolishing and disposing the debris also incurs costs.

Hierarchy of Design: Renovation Edition

Although your neighborhood, lot, and floor plan are already in place, changes should be confirmed in order of their hierarchy before embarking on a renovation. Decisions made in order of their influence (changeability) save time and allow for responsible, big-picture to small-picture solutions. The feasibility of a renovation hinges upon addressing the possibilities in order of logical importance. The level of difficulty required to change an item is the metric I use. The more difficult, or impossible, an item is to change, the higher its hierarchy, and the earlier it should be decided. For example, property lines are more difficult to change than is extending an existing roofline, changing the architectural style, expanding into the attic, or replacing cabinets.

Smaller decisions (easier to change) should occur only after larger decisions (harder to change) have been made. Your personal sanity, your family, and your contractor will appreciate this approach. But even the smaller decisions become hard to change after they are installed. Deciding between a good and a bad option is easy. Wrenching decisions are those that must be made between equally good choices, as, for example, picking the paint color for one room to add to an overall décor and yet remain distinctive. There are so many beautiful colors and materials available. How can anyone decide without going into a decision paralysis? The same example holds for selecting countertop, splash, and floor materials. These are all important decisions, but they do not affect the size of the rooms, the style of the architecture, or the location of the property line. Get assistance on these decisions from your architect and interior designer.

Some lovely homes have unfortunate locations (hard to change; if only they had built somewhere else!), and many wonderful locations have unfortunate homes (easier to change with renovations). Likewise, a beautiful exterior can have an unworkable floor plan, or a delightful floor plan can be wrapped with an uninspired exterior. How do you decide what to do first? Fix the façade or improve the floor plan? My recommendation is to follow the hierarchy of decisions as far as your budget will allow. Perfection across the board is as rare as it is expensive. Improving the curb appeal is less important to me than is a workable floor plan. This is because when a house is comfortable for your lifestyle, your desire is to stay put. If current budgets do not allow, improving the curb appeal can wait for a later renovation.

The following steps are similar to those mentioned in Chapter 3 but also include issues specific to existing houses. The most important considerations in my list are the ones that are most difficult, if not impossible, to change. Unchangeable items are the big considerations and must come first. All lesser possibilities, although important, do not have the power to remedy the bigger issues. Save those until later.

STEP 1: CONFIRM YOUR NEIGHBORHOOD

The first decision is to confirm you want to live in your existing neighborhood. I can't emphasize enough the importance of living in a place that appeals to you and your lifestyle. Why? Neighborhoods are complex to create and harder to change. Moving to a house in a different subdivision may disrupt more of your living patterns than your new house can counterbalance. One house alone, no matter how perfect, cannot change the character of an entire neighborhood. See Chapter 3 for my recommendations for objectively judging whether a neighborhood is your best fit.

STEP 2: DETERMINE THE BUILDABLE AREA WITHIN YOUR PROPERTY

Zoning setbacks, neighborhood covenants, and utility servitudes all combine to limit the property area on which you can build. Buildable area is not all of the green you maintain. Without obtaining a setback variance or additional property, many additions will extend past those lines so are not feasible. Determining expansion possibilities starts with reviewing the survey, locating property lines, house footprint, building lines, and unbuildable servitudes.

STEP 3: DETERMINE ROOF PLAN EXTENDIBILITY

Unless covered with flat roofs, the roof slopes also affect the feasibility of additions. Understand the geometry of your existing roof, its ridges and its valleys, to explore

An existing front door continues to welcome family and guests to an updated and expanded interior.

the options of extendibility. Complicated, multifaceted shapes limit easy connections. Simple gables, by comparison, lend themselves to cross-gabled or shed extensions. Louisiana's abundant rainfall makes unrestricted roof drainage a major consideration. Extensions must re-

The Kevin Harris Rules of Renovation

I have three hard and fast rules that I share with my renovation clients:

Rule 1: Renovation of a kitchen + master bathroom = move out. If you plan to renovate both kitchen and master bathroom simultaneously, you *must* find somewhere else to live during construction. Yes, *must*! You can't simply live in the other parts of the home. When only renovating a kitchen, the family can eat out more or camp out with a makeshift kitchen. When they are without the master bathroom, parents can share a bathroom with the kids. Each improvement comes with a level of inconvenience and requisite demand for tolerance. However, when both master bathroom and kitchen are out of commission, even the most skilled campers and the most sharing parents behave differently. In my experience, this level of inconvenience causes great strain and often results in collateral damage to your family, pets, architect, contractor, and innocent bystanders. A renovation can, and

solve the functional and aesthetic integration between new and existing.

STEP 4: DETERMINE INSIDE/ OUTSIDE CONNECTIONS

How does your existing plan connect with the exterior? Study approaches to and from the street, garage, and outdoor living areas. Adding a room may require alternative interfaces with the exteriors. Windows provide views and natural light, and doors allow passage. When exploring possible extensions, be cautious of creating bedrooms without windows. Codes require bedrooms to have emergency access.

Floor plans should flow well with your lifestyle for exterior living. A common renovation challenge is correcting this flow in pre-1940 homes in which open windows limit family privacy, living spaces are located near the social interaction of the street, and bedrooms line the rear yard, which is an additional playground accessible through the kitchen. Air conditioning and lifestyle evolution now flip these arrangements. Windows are closed and houses are more private. Street yards are manicured but without exterior living, which has relocated to a spacious and private backyard.

Given these conditions, a renovation can delightfully repurpose those arrangements and expand the living spaces while balancing the requirements for access, and views. Simply because the house lacks the amenities of a new master suite, open den/kitchen, or doors to a new pool, outdoor living, or kitchen, should not eliminate your renovating an older house in a great location.

Typical connections to consider include:

- *Bedrooms:* Building codes mandate minimum-sized, operable windows for each bedroom for egress in the event of a fire.

- *Living room/den:* Living patterns suggest views and ready access from these spaces directly to the areas for exterior living.

- *Automobiles:* Covered parking and enclosed garage parking directly accessible to the main house has replaced the detached garage. Off-street guest parking accommodations are required by many subdivisions and zoning codes.

- *Storage:* Provisions should be made for securely and accessibly storing a boat, golf cart, four wheeler, bicycles, or yard tools.

- *Outdoor living:* Another consideration is covered areas adjacent to the swimming pool, back yard, or outdoor kitchen that are readily accessible to the main kitchen, living room, and den.

- *Driveway access:* Paved areas should connect the garage with the street. This is usually

should be, a dynamic and enjoyable process. But when adults are denied the simple pleasures of master bathroom privacy, compounded with the inconvenience of a kitchenless home, the process ceases to be enjoyable. So buck up and make alternative living arrangements.

Rule 2: Never race a baby. One motivator that drives the enlargement of an existing home is the accommodation of an additional family member. This holds true for in-laws as well as for infants. However, my advice is to never race a baby. The baby always wins. Here is my logic: Human gestation takes nine months and is divided into trimesters. The time between discovering a new baby is arriving and deciding to expand usually consumes the first trimester. All seems well. You then select an architect, approve a design, have drawings prepared, and obtain estimates. Demolition commences by the end of the second trimester. The expectant mother is now in her third trimester, which obstetricians jokingly refer to as the nesting phase. All of our advanced technology, communications, and ability to create comfortable environments are no match for competing with natural forces. Just when the demolition crew begins to bust out walls, creating dust, and generally making a huge mess, Mother Nature's influence demands tidying up in preparation for the new baby. The contractor has lost the battle before he has begun. Racing construction against a baby's arrival is, predictably, a no-win situation. My advice is to either postpone the start of construction, or grab a comfortable seat to watch the pending fireworks. As the old saying goes, "It's not nice to fool Mother Nature."

Rule 3: Design must involve coherence. Any additions must be integrated into what already exists to form a coherent new whole. This is in contrast to the common practice of designing each addition as an independent expression, unrelated to, or challenging the design integrity of, the original. In short, I believe that the end result of a renovation should simply be a bigger, better house in which the distinction between old and new is difficult for the casual observer to identify. In some ways, this process is comparable to good plastic surgery: an artistic repair, alteration, or enhancement that both respects and beautifies an existing living structure. To use a storybook example, in contrast to rule 3, the infamous surgeon Dr. Frankenstein may have been a genius, but his creation is referred to as a monster.

the largest paved area other than that of the floor slab.

STEP 5: IDENTIFY FLOOR PLAN PROBLEMS

Ask yourself which aspects of your current floor plan you do not like. Which rooms are too small, too dark, in the wrong place, or separated from related living areas?

STEP 6: IDENTIFY NEEDS AND WANTS, THE INITIAL SCOPE OF WORK

The needs and wants your forever home should satisfy form your initial renovation scope of work, in performance terms. Enlarging a utility room, renovating a kitchen, adding a master suite, creating a home office, media room, or outdoor kitch-

en—your answers to considerations of this type guide what to improve.

STEP 7: IDENTIFY ACTIVITIES THAT CAN SHARE SPACE

The quickest method to reduce the size of your additions is to have multipurpose spaces, where possible. For example, outfitting a living room to also serve as the media room or a cabana to periodically serve as a guest suite can minimize what needs to be built.

STEP 8: IDENTIFY EXISTING UNDERUSED OR UNUSED SPACES

Before embarking on an addition, conduct an audit to illuminate those areas rarely used and no longer supporting your lifestyle. These should be considered as resources for repurposing to serve current needs. Consider the dining or formal living room that is rarely used. The location and lack of use of such rooms make each a prime target for repurposing into a music room, home office, or, by removing walls, a breakfast room open to the kitchen. Rethinking the usage and layout of existing rooms often reduces construction needed for successful renovations.

STEP 9: EXPLORE CREATIVE OPTIONS

Assembling the information, opportunities, and constraints from items 1–8 above, your architect is now prepared to efficiently and creatively explore feasible options to convert an existing house into your forever home. One key to a successful and cost-effective renovation is to leave as much of what already exists, and to minimize the areas modified or added.

STEP 10: PERFECT YOUR STYLE

Style enters the renovation process at the end, the same as it does with new construction. I recommend bringing the final style into consideration only after determining a desirable floor plan. See Chapter 2 for more on style files. Once major parts are in the plan, the plastic surgery component of renovation design can blend into, enhance, or completely change an existing style.

Common Problems Renovations Solve

New houses come equipped with up-to-date kitchens and luxurious baths and have the sparkle of newness. Existing homes seldom offer the same conveniences that the building profession touts as being indispensable—that is, unless one contemplates an addition or a renovation.

Room arrangement: Room locations in older houses are often at odds with suburban life today. Living spaces are on the front, while bedrooms line the back, limiting access from inside the house to the

> "Many cramped and inconvenient cottages transform into open and efficient homes. In many cases, most of the space is available for creative alteration."

backyard, pool, and barbecue. Views of these social spaces are from bedrooms and a kitchen window. Rethinking the arrangement of rooms within a home will completely change the use, spirit, feel, and energy of the overall living environment. For example, consider repurposing the current room functions to open a main living area onto the back yard. Toss away the old labels for existing rooms. Simply because a room was used for formal dining does not prevent its use as playroom, music room, or library/study. Consider converting the old master bedroom into a new kitchen when its location abuts the major living spaces. Many cramped and inconvenient cottages transform into open and efficient homes. In many cases, most of the space needed is under the existing roof and available for creative alteration.

Flow: Busier lifestyles demand multitasking, and your home should facilitate ready circulation between concurrent activities. Single use, dead-end spaces choke off this flow. Consider circulation options and additional doorways. Locate the kitchen so it is adjacent but removed from traffic. Otherwise, an efficient kitchen becomes a hallway that interrupts the cook and frustrates socializing guests.

One flow test is to observe how your guests circulate during a party and where they tend to gather. How does your house function under increased traffic? Arrangements that operate efficiently under the added stress of large groups of family and guests will perform exceptionally well under normal daily loads.

Exterior connections: Explore multiple, well-placed connections to the exterior. A home is not a self-contained spaceship, where exterior walks are possible but difficult. It is, rather, part of a larger whole that includes the surrounding landscape. Accessibility to exterior "rooms" enlarges entertainment capacity and reconnects your family with nature.

Incompatible additions: Many homes come with ill-planned additions that are not designed to endure the elements and detract from the original. Remodeling can correct those annoying aspects and "make things right." However, a set-aside contingency should be included in the plan in order to cover "behind-the-wall" surprises. Not all houses are built alike.

Unfortunate curb "appeal": Curing the "uglies" of previous misguided efforts is a great way to increase the desirability of a home. This requires artistic intuition and careful analysis. The artful cutting away of, or adding to, an existing home can correct an unfortunate curb "appeal" and reinvent its character. Seasoned design professionals excel with this visual metric. Adjustments can correct awkward proportions, complete unbalanced compositions, and adjust the primary focus.

Recording Existing Conditions

If you decide to pursue your project following the design consultation, recording the existing conditions comes before any detailed drawings are prepared. Renovations interface with existing structures, systems, and details. These must all be identified in sufficient detail for the architect to prepare the drawings to safely guide the craftsmen. For example, blindly removing what turns out to be a bearing wall can be a matter of life and death. Knowing what structural systems are in place facilitates the design for an alternative means of load transfer (i.e., a column, beam, or hidden truss).

A large island anchors a kitchen, stages homework, cookie decorating, crafts and drinks with friends. Bookmatched openings connect the kitchen to the drop zone and laundry on one side and the butler's pantry on the other.

CHAPTER SEVEN

That Four-Letter Word: Cost

> *"Sometimes one pays most for the things one gets for nothing."*
>
> —ALBERT EINSTEIN

ven the renowned physicist rediscovered the ancient truth of *caveat emptor* (Latin, *let the buyer beware*), the warning to examine and judge a product or service before purchase, and he added his observation that free things maintain balance with universal reciprocity. The vernacular saying, "There ain't no such thing as a free lunch," also refers to this economic axiom. The maxim originated when saloons offered lunches to attract patrons. When patrons bought a drink, their lunch was on the house. Menus of salted ham, cheese, and crackers, de-

signed to increase thirst, boosted beer purchases. The lesson is clear: when something appears free, hidden costs are likely attached.

The Four Variables

The four variables of project management are scope of work, time, cost, and quality. Most start with a defined scope of work and must balance the three remaining variables of time, cost, and quality. Try as you may, it is impossible to optimize all of them. You can directly influence two, but all four are interconnected in constant balance. Adjusting one affects the others. The Iron Triangle diagram on the next page illustrates how these variables interplay.

It is important to understand these variables and how each responds to changes. Not unlike Professor Einstein's universe, balance will be sustained.

For a family with Louisiana ties, the elements of salvaged beams and whitewashed bricks deliver a dose of vernacular culture to a formal dining room.

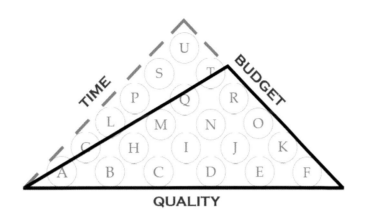

In casual jargon this triangle is oft stated as "Time, price, or quality. Pick any two." As with any triangle enclosing a predefined area, adjusting one leg will affect the lengths of the other two. Imagine each side as a project variable. For example, if your goal is for high quality and low cost, then adding time restores the balance. Alternatively, if shorter time and high quality is paramount, then cost must increase. Choosing to limit two legs—for example, time and cost—necessitates reducing the area enclosed, the scope of work.

➤ *Scope of work:* This is what construction is required to satisfy in terms of desired outcomes, standards, and cost. Scope is the area inside the iron triangle. Adjusting this quantity directly affects the three enclosing legs, your remaining variables.

➤ *Time:* This is the time from design through construction. Several forces influence time independently of the desire to move quickly. For example, adequate time must be allowed for the architect to responsibly produce plans,

and the contractor's fiduciary need to balance available time and tasks with workers allocated to your project must also be taken into account. Increasing time lengthens that leg of the triangle.

➤ *Cost:* This includes your budget, architectural fees, and charges for your contractor and materials. Reducing your budget shortens this leg.

➤ *Quality:* This can be defined as the subjective ability to perform satisfactorily in service and be suited for its intended purpose. Not all quality extends the budget, but budget and cost directly affect the quality achievable.

Life Cycle Cost Factor

There are initial costs and life cycle costs to home ownership. Your home is likely your most valuable and largest capital investment. All savings on initial costs are available elsewhere. However, consider the repercussions of any construction reductions against the life cycle costs over a 15- to 30-year cycle.

Facility managers recognize that 70 percent of ownership costs originate from the operational costs of maintenance, repairs, and utilities. Construction expenses reflect only 20 percent of total ownership costs. Financing is at 6 percent, and design and engineering fees round out the final 3 percent. Hence, over time, your biggest savings potential lies in designing your forever home to minimize the operational and maintenance costs.

Below are ways homeowners can save money during the building process, along with my recommendations to responsibly limit project costs.

Negotiated Bid Process

The traditional method is to prepare detailed drawings and solicit bids from a handful of reputable general contractors. However, I believe a different approach to negotiating the bid provides more accurate pricing during the design decision process and better suits homeowner requirements.

Before preparing the final drawings, I recommend selecting a contractor to work with the architect and to provide a more accurate "probable pricing" of the schematic design. This pricing effort should include the major subcontractors. Access to probable cost information is paramount to deciding what to include relative to a budget. Obtaining costs from actual craftsmen will educate a more informed decision process. Once the final drawings are completed, instead of bidding multiple general contractors, my process promotes bidding individual subcontractors.

This design-build method provides cost guidance at appropriate times for decision making. The first price check follows design development review and subcontractor pricing of the schematics. These drawings define the general scope of work in enough detail for preliminary estimates. Components that dominate the budget are quantified. Allowances for finishes, fixtures, and appliances determine your probable budget. Using this model, the contractor, subcontractors, and material

The butler's pantry quietly stages functions between the kitchen and dining room while freeing kitchen countertops from the clutter of countertop appliances.

suppliers are consulted before all details have been decided. This enables "probable" but reasonably accurate cost feedback to inform your selection decisions, putting you in the driver's seat, controlling costs.

Whenever preliminary costs mandate trimming the scope of work, these estimates inform possible compromises to be included in the construction details. A

Well thought cabinet and appliance placement make cooking in this powerhouse kitchen a delight.

second estimate based on the final drawings, with several dozen line items, lends even greater granularity to identifying each cost. It assists in confirming that all elements were included and clarifies any items to be rebid or negotiated prior to contract signing.

Remember the iron triangle in which three variables enclose the scope of work. Adding scope increases the area enclosed and directly affects cost, quality, and time. When negotiating this way, your contractor becomes an advocate and a valuable asset in your search for the best price for any scope of work.

Design

"If you think it's expensive to hire a professional to do the job, wait until you hire an amateur."

—RED ADAIR,
OIL WELL FIREFIGHTER, 1915-2004

Early in my career, a prospective client shared a catalogue of 1,200 house plans. Taking a deep breath, I flipped through and noticed that several plans had been earmarked for reference. Each had some merit but included features or attributes conflicting with my understanding of the client's desires. The more plans I reviewed, the less intimidated I became. Finally, I looked up and inquired with a smile, "With so many inexpensive plans to choose from, why do you need me?" She admitted, in frustration, that the 1,200 options did not resolve even half of her needs. She called after realizing professional assistance was necessary to craft a plan containing everything she would require.

One of the initial expenses of achieving your forever home is the cost of the drawings. How the design functions or accommodates your day-to-day activities is an architectural rather than contractor issue. These intangibles should guide what is drawn and what is drawn defines how the house should be built, using specific materials. The tangible common to every house is a set of drawings. And that begs the questions (1) why not lower these costs from the beginning? and (2) why hire an expensive architect, especially when every newsstand advertises sets of house plans for less than the cost of a mattress?

Homeowners resist contacting an architect because of their uncertainty over, or fear of, the added cost. Espe-cially when planning a forever home, working with an architect is a necessary investment that will pay dividends galore. If this seems counterintuitive, it helps to understand that a good architect will help you

➢ get the design right the first time, avoiding costly mid-project changes;

➢ help you through construction negotiations, which usually results in substantial savings by reducing scope of work unknowns, and eliminating items that, given their price, you feel you can do without; and

➢ guide the project from start to finish, ensuring all is done to your expectations, so you receive the house for what it costs to construct.

The most important aspect about obtaining a forever home is in knowing what and how to build. Unless you have knowledge of both construction and drafting, or you happen to find an acceptable solution in a catalogue, you will need assistance in design and creating the necessary drawings.

In Chapter 1 I go into detail on how to evaluate options to find the service level right for you. The services of an architect are not needed for many homes. However, for those that do, I cover how to interview and select an architect and describe in greater detail the value an architect can bring to your forever home.

Procuring a design and drawings from an architect is the most expensive service provider option but can also result in savings that exceed the added expense, and it is the most likely route to achieving your forever home. Using an architect is one of the few alternatives offering guidance and participation through construction. Less expensive drawings are obtainable from plan services or magazines, but these don't provide the legal responsibility of a licensed architect. One exception is the architect who is also a design builder. Contractors are liable for what they build, regardless of who prepares the drawings. Architects are liable for what they draw. Hav-

ing both on your project lessens your exposure should something go wrong.

Most of my clients have been drawn either to builders offering limited customizations to standard plans, or other less expensive service providers, only to realize that those efforts failed to deliver the desired results. They decided to hire an architect only after multiple unsuccessful attempts that avoided the initial drawing expense. Hoping subsequent iterations would result in their forever home, each revealed more and more that they were not able, on their own, to arrange and design things to their liking. These experiences helped them recognize the value of professional assistance. I am usually commissioned for the third (or fourth) attempt, when it becomes more important to get it right.

I like to put design fees in perspective with other typical household expenditures. For example, for the cost of a modest luxury automobile (that will depreciate greatly over time), a homeowner can create a personal haven that most often appreciates over time. Imagine selling

As with any professional, the lowest priced is not always the best. The adage is correct: you simply get what you pay for.

your car, after 200,000 miles, for more than you initially paid for it. For a renovation, the investment in design fees may be equivalent to the cost of new den furniture, but will improve the quality of life for your family and increase in value.

As with any professional, the lowest priced is not always the best. Seldom do we want the cheapest surgeon to perform a delicate operation or expect gourmet cuisine from a hamburger cook. The adage is correct: you simply get what you pay for. In making your selection, carefully inspect and compare credentials, expertise, experience, and reputation to determine worth and if there is potential for a comfortable fit. Keep in mind that not every architect is the best choice for you, and you are not the best client for every architect. I cannot overemphasize the importance of selecting an architect who feels right for you, and you should expect to pay accordingly for greater experience and reputation.

General Contractor

Contractors charge profit and overhead fees in addition to the cost of materials and labor. One extreme method of cost reduction is to self-perform and become your own contractor. My recommendation, however, is to understand what factors influence these fees before you decide.

DO IT YOURSELF

Many attempt to save by acting as their own general contractor (GC). Plenty of support exists for the idea of building your own house. Do-It-Yourself (DIY) schools are located across the country, numerous books pontificate on the subject, and an endless supply of available workers stand idle outside big-box, home-improvement stores, waiting to be asked to work that day. With all of the positive hype, why not consider DIY as an option?

Experience has provided me with a simple answer. Yes, you can build your own house or even perform part of its construction, but you don't save. Rather, you will earn every nickel. You can do the painting yourself, for example, and reduce your labor bill. But realize this is at the expense of your own labor. You will be exchanging a cash investment for sweat equity to accomplish your goals. Unfortunately, the supply of both is limited.

No one today actually builds a home by himself or herself. Building codes require licensed subcontractors for plumbing, electrical, and air conditioning work, leaving the rest of the job—the bulk of the work, and its coordination—up to you. If you don't feel comfortable swinging a hammer or wielding a saw, you can hire out the physical labor and limit your role to the administrative elements. And in so doing, you can save the expense of

A raised counter provides a remote perch for guests to interact without interfering.

Outdoor kitchens function at their best when communicating visually and physically with their indoor counterparts.

the contractor's profit and overhead in exchange for your time required to organize, supply, and supervise the operation. The work does not operate on automatic pilot.

Someone—the GC, typically—must schedule all of the activities, make adjustments whenever materials or workers don't show up when expected, or when materials and people do arrive onsite, but are damaged or otherwise not working properly. And then there are the unexpected expenses of your construction education, which includes mastering the learning curve of discerning good workers, bad deals, and how best to sequence activities. Each lesson increases your costs and construction time. When work that has been completed must be removed, replaced, or rebuilt, it's the GC's responsibility to spot the mistakes early and ensure everything gets done right. As I said, you will earn every nickel you want to save. Contractors work very hard for their fees.

I have witnessed successful projects in which the owner also acted as the general contractor, but in these situations the project scope was small or limited and very well-defined; the homeowner had extensive experience in construction; intimate access (father-in-law, sister, retired uncle) to someone with extensive experience in construction and was willing to commit the time to support that person through the process; or the homeowner had limited construction experience but had incredibly good accounting, human relations, and project management skills, with the willingness, time, and temperament to see a project lasting 6 to 18 months through to completion.

GC OVERHEAD AND PROFIT

If the time commitment and risk inherent in self-contracting is not for you, I strongly suggest selecting a qualified general contractor. In exchange for the fees, your project will benefit from the GC's knowledge, expertise, materials sources, and network of subcontractors. The actual amount is, typically, broken into overhead and profit. In my 30-plus years of practice, I have rarely seen a reputable or experienced contractor charge outside the rates generally charged in any community. However, it is not unusual to see higher percentage fees for smaller projects. These often cost more because they lack any economy of scale. For example, it takes just as long to travel to and inspect work on a small renovation as to direct incremental progress on a new house.

In Chapter 4 I discuss in detail how to find and select a contractor. Just as with your architect or designer, be-ware of shopping for price. This is especially true when one price is out of line with the competition. Should you choose to go with the lowest-priced GC, it will be up to you to confirm that everything is included in the scope of work, and at the quality level you expect. Horror stories abound about construction projects gone awry, in which the owner was repeatedly informed that desired items were "not included," and the GC was ever on the lookout for an opportunity to cut a corner, adding surprise change orders, or failing to pay the subcontractors (only discovered after liens were filed on the home). For those homeowners who want to focus primarily on how long their house will take to build, I advise similar caution, as there is a likely correlation between fast and dirty (shoddy) work and accelerated completion. Learn from history and the story of the free lunch bargain. For the inexperienced DIY contractor, the final cost of constant construction education headaches and resultant work do-overs (whenever caught in time), will most likely exceed any perceived savings.

Being a GC is a business providing a service in exchange for compensation and a bit of profit. I want contractors to have this profit motive, but charge a fair price.

Subcontractors

Everyone with a "honey-do" list of home maintenance repairs has some DIY experience. While taking on the more difficult subcontractor jobs yourself is likely out of the question, you might be considering performing the seemingly lesser tasks of painting or site cleanup on your own. At the very least, this could help reduce those costs in a long list of expenses. That is the upside.

Here's the downside. This approach can be loaded with problems. Waiting for evenings and weekends to do your part can bring the entire construction schedule to a sudden halt. When a job you are performing is delayed, your untimely completion can cause a domino effect on other craftsmen scheduled to follow your work. Scrambling to salvage their unfilled workdays, they must move on to other job sites and not simply wait on the sidelines for you to finish. Once on another job, they must fulfill those obligations before returning to your project. These delays can cascade uncontrollably throughout your entire construction and result in increased time as well as costs.

For example, perhaps you do your own home theater installation but delay installing the wiring until the drywall is scheduled to be installed. Your contractor can either stop construction until you get around to running wires in the walls and ceilings or keep to the schedule and hold the drywall subcontractor to his agreement to install on time. If the drywall is installed, the studs and joists are no longer exposed and you likely do not have the skills or tools to install hidden wires or equipment supports under retrofit conditions. Because the wire installation missed its window of opportunity, later installation becomes more involved. There is additional work for your electrician (to fish wires through walls and ceilings), your wallboard finisher (to repair the access holes created by the elec-

"For the inexperienced DIY contractor, the final cost of constant construction education headaches and resultant work do-overs will most likely exceed any perceived savings."

trician), and your painter (for repainting the repaired wallboard). If your contractor keeps to the schedule, and you still want theater systems installed, expect a bill for the additional work. It's usually straightforward for the GC to schedule and sequence each subcontractor—that is, unless you are in the middle, wearing the hat of a subcontractor in addition to that of an owner.

In addition to sequencing issues, there are a maddening number of instances in which the work of one subcontractor overlaps, or interfaces, with another, often resulting in finger pointing back and forth as each side claims that a problem was not their fault, or not included in their contracted scope of work. This can put you in a vulnerable position. Here is one actual example I witnessed. The owner decided to paint the walls. By the time he showed up with painting supplies, the higher wall area was no longer accessible. The scaffolding used to install the drywall and finish the trim had been dismantled by the drywall subcontractor and moved to another work site. The paint subcontractor (owner) was now responsible for his own equipment to access the area he wanted to paint. Unfortunately, he neglected to coordinate his use of the scaffolding with either the contractor or drywall subcontractor.

Materials

> "I only sell cheap paint to my rich customers. They are the only ones who can afford to repaint."
>
> —JOSEPH KLIMCZAK, MY WISE FATHER-IN-LAW AND FORMER OWNER OF J. K. HARDWARE, BOGALUSA, LA

Of all the ways to cut costs on your forever home, attempting to save on the materials is often the most counterproductive. Sure, there's always a special offer, an overstock, an advertised factory second that promises to save you money. But businesses that sell cheap materials are in it to make a profit, so consider carefully what these "opportunities" really offer.

Unfortunately, over the years, I have witnessed deal after golden deal go sour once the materials arrived. These cheap/discounted materials included "bargain" stone tiles that were out of square and uneven in thickness (requiring each stone to be recut); hardwood flooring with misaligned tongues and grooves (resulting in a cheese-grater surface that was hazardous to bare feet); plumbing fixtures that were missing critical parts; and salvaged lumber soaked in hazardous preservatives or soaked with machinery oil. This unbelievable "deal" came from an old sewing factory floor. The embedded oils hidden in the wood grain would not accept a finish. The wood was subsequently removed and replaced. In each of these cases, far more was spent correcting the problems than it would have cost to initially buy quality materials.

Cost-saving backfires are not always the norm, but unfortunate results happen often enough to raise serious concern. My advice before you make an acquisition is to know the provenance—the specifications and history, the nitty-gritty details—of any material you intend to purchase yourself; know who you are purchasing it from, and examine the offers closely with your contractor and architect for potential repercussions and hidden expenses.

The proven way to save on materials is to work with trusted professionals, buy from reputable distributors, and do your homework. Trust but verify.

Caution: The Friends and Family Discount

Whenever you mention constructing your own home, expect offers for "a good deal" from an uncle, cousin, friend from the soccer field, or anyone you know who works in some aspect of the construction trade. This can work to your benefit, but before attempting to take advantage of these apparent opportunities, consider the origin of the savings and the possible costs to the relationship and your project.

Is your relationship with the person making the offer so close that it warrants a "deal" of that magnitude? Are there any strings attached? Will the deal require pocket-lining expenses down the road (think inexpensive phone but high monthly service)? Is it pos-

This family's elegant, fun personality is celebrated with a formal Versailles pattern of stone and wood parquettes below the whimsical repetition of façade windows.

Warehouse timbers replace walls in this renovation to accommodate a wide open floor plan.

sible that the person offering the deal is hoping to leverage the discount or gift for future favors?

The friend does not always share your notion of quality, price, or what constitutes "a good deal." If you avail yourself of the deal (materials or labor), consider what happens when timeliness or quality does not meet expectations. How will the relationship alter or change if the gift is rejected or replaced? What is the potential

emotional fallout from misaligned expectations? Are your prepared to take the risk and expense of a do-over?

Each construction site operates on a hierarchy of relationships that form the chain of command. The craftsmen work for their foremen, and their foremen work for the subcontractor, who works for the general contractor, who in turn works for the owner but takes directions from the architect, who also works for the owner. Note that the top of this pyramid is always you, the owner. Everyone ultimately is working for you. It is your house, and it is you who is paying the bills. When inserting another player into this structured hierarchy, especially when it is someone who has your favor and ear, it can undermine the chain of command and disrupt the entire process.

For example, one client took advantage of an offer of free labor from an uncle who was an electrician. When scheduling conflicts started to heat up with the GC over delays in the electrical work, the uncle responded by jumping rank and complaining directly to his niece, the homeowner. Fortunately, we were involved and immediately consulted with both the contractor and the uncle. We found out the uncle's workforce was fully committed with existing work and could not reliably schedule ample craftsmen to work his niece's "deal." To reach an amicable solution, we obtained a fair bid and gave the uncle first right of refusal on the subcontract. The uncle passed on the work. Keeping business as business allowed the contractor to complete the project on time, the uncle to save face with his niece, and his niece, the owner, to not be caught in the middle.

Caution: The Might-as-Well ("Midas") Touch

A surefire way to save money during construction is to avoid the might-as-well ("Midas") touch. This occurs whenever owners visit their building sites and innocently invoke those most costly words ever spoken in construction, "While you're here, you might as well..." I know how tempting it can be, and appreciate the seductive power of making such a statement and witnessing the results. But uttering those words increases the scope of work, which increases the price and thwarts your previous efforts at cost control. Might-as-well directives cost real gold and will consume even the most generous construction budgets.

Caution: Timing

The most expensive time to make a change is during construction. The best time is while your house is still on paper. There will always be some changes during custom residential projects. The important thing to do is to consciously limit them.

Caution: Indecision Costs

Throughout a project, you will be asked to make decisions on various options. The options and the materials you select obviously impact your costs. However, many owners do not realize that the failure to make timely decisions will also add costs.

As discussed in Chapter 5, construction is a linear process in which one task builds on another. When an owner delays making timely decisions, an unpleasant "train wreck" of scheduling happens. For example, suppose you authorize construction but remain undecided on the bathroom flooring. That decision is not required until it's time to install the bathroom tiles (before plumbing fixtures are installed). Oops! The long-awaited perfect flooring selection is available, but is a special order item with a 12-week delivery schedule. What to do now? None of the options are ideal: halt work and have the contractor remobilize his subs in three months; select from previously rejected but readily available alternatives; pay a premium to have materials air freighted, drop-shipped, or personally picked up and delivered; or a combination of any of these. I have seen them all.

No one wants to upset or nag you, the owner, or get on the wrong side of your check-writing self. Make it easier on yourself and your pocketbook and confirm material lead times and final dates for selection delivery onsite.

Don't Feed the Bears

I usually advise clients to treat their construction site as if were a national park, where signs warn, "Do Not Feed the Bears." It's something I learned from a gracious woman who allowed her better nature to rule over common sense. She firmly believed that you get more in life with exceptional kindness and chose to practice this on the carpenters. Every morning, the contractor would show up and direct the men on that day's work. Then he would leave to attend to other projects. Almost every day, around 10:00 a.m., the homeowner would call a break and share fresh-baked cookies and milk with the "hard-working men." This unscheduled social break was much appreciated by the workers. However, instead of motivating a higher level of craftsmanship for the minor cost of cookies and milk, this gift ended up costing the homeowner thousands of dollars in overtime charges. Those "hard-working men" were being paid hourly, and the contract was on a cost-plus basis. The cause of this spike in labor expense was not discovered until after the milk-and-cookie guests had moved on to other projects. Paying wages out of pocket and with no simple fix, the owner realized too late how expensive those free cookies were.

Kevin's Top Three Ways to Save

Besides what is mentioned above, my top three ways to save are to consider life cycle costs, right-size your floor plan, and make the house your forever home.

Life cycle costs: As mentioned at the start of this chapter, the greatest potential savings is to design your home to reduce the maintenance and operating costs that account for 70 percent of the total life cycle expenditures. For example, cladding the exteriors with low-maintenance materials that hold paint and resist rot, and installing additional insulation along with high-efficiency air conditioners will reduce annual repairs and utility bills.

Right sizing: The second savings potential is "right-sizing" your scope of work: you can save by simply building what you need and making it only as large as your lifestyle requires. Many spaces can be designed for multiple functions, thus lessening square-footage requirements. I recently designed a home where the owner was interested in making space for a future elevator. I decided to enlarge and place the wine cellar in direct alignment with a larger, second-floor guest closet. This allowed full and current use of the spaces while also allowing for a future elevator. The plan anticipated this element, its unique framing and electrical requirements, along with convenient access to and from the future unit. The wine cellar could easily convert to a smaller wet bar adjacent to the elevator and provide an aesthetic nook concealing the elevator. The guest closet would become a bit shallower and back up to an elevator shaft. The elevator door would open onto a second-floor hallway, providing second-floor access without compromising bedroom privacy or entirely eliminating needed closet space.

Build for the long term: Finally, building a forever home is, in itself, a great way to save, as it implies that you have stopped relocating. According to the Tax Policy Center, for homes owned less than four years, transaction costs are the largest single expense. These exceed mortgage interest payments, property taxes, and any profit you might earn from increased home equity. Even when you live in a home for 11 years, these costs can total 20 percent of the entire cost of ownership. There can be a real dollar value to staying in one place. Whenever living in a forever home, you want to stay put, and you'll save big!

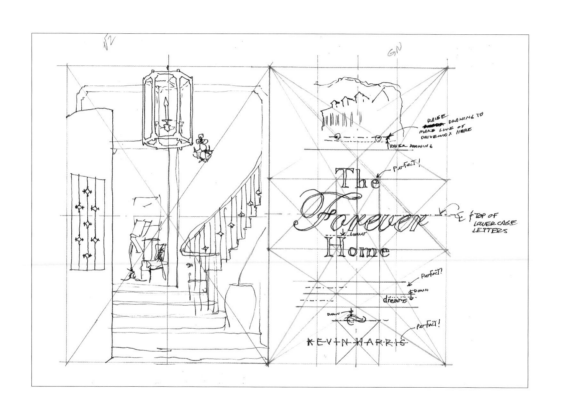